Building your own PC

A guide for beginners

December 2024

By Dr Alex Bugeja, PhD

Introduction

Chapter 1 Understanding PC Components: A Beginner's Overview

Chapter 2 Choosing the Right Processor (CPU) for Your Needs

Chapter 3 Motherboards: The Foundation of Your Build

Chapter 4 All About RAM: Understanding Memory Types and Speeds

Chapter 5 Graphics Cards (GPU): A Deep Dive for Visual Performance

Chapter 6 Storage Solutions: HDD vs. SSD vs. NVMe

Chapter 7 Power Supplies (PSU): Fueling Your System Safely

Chapter 8 Cases: Aesthetics, Airflow, and Size Considerations

Chapter 9 Cooling Solutions: Keeping Your PC Temperatures in Check

Chapter 10 Essential Tools and Workspace Preparation

Chapter 11 Installing the Motherboard and CPU

Chapter 12 Mounting the CPU Cooler

Chapter 13 Installing RAM Modules

Chapter 14 Installing the Graphics Card

Chapter 15 Mounting Storage Devices

Chapter 16 Connecting the Power Supply

Chapter 17 Internal Cable Management: A Clean Build is a Happy Build

Chapter 18 Installing the Operating System (OS)

Chapter 19 Installing Drivers and Essential Software

Chapter 20 Basic BIOS/UEFI Configuration

Chapter 21 Testing and Troubleshooting Your Build

Chapter 22 Overclocking: Risks and Rewards (Optional)

Chapter 23 Peripherals: Choosing Keyboards, Mice, and Monitors

Chapter 24 Upgrading Your PC in the Future

Chapter 25 Maintaining Your PC: Cleaning and Optimization

Introduction

Welcome to the exciting world of PC building! If you've ever felt intimidated by the prospect of assembling your own computer, fear not. This book is designed to guide you, the absolute beginner, through every step of the process, transforming you from a novice to a confident PC builder.

Building your own PC might seem like a daunting task, reserved for tech wizards and seasoned enthusiasts. But the truth is, with the right guidance and a little patience, anyone can do it. In fact, building your own computer is not only achievable but also incredibly rewarding.

Why Build Your Own PC?

You might be wondering, "Why bother building a PC when I can just buy a pre-built one?" That's a valid question, and the answer comes down to several key advantages:

- **Customization:** Building your own PC allows you to tailor every single component to your specific needs and preferences. Whether you're a hardcore gamer, a content creator, or simply need a reliable machine for everyday tasks, you have complete control over the hardware that goes into your system. This level of customization is simply not possible with pre-built systems.

- **Performance:** By carefully selecting each component, you can ensure that your PC delivers the exact level of performance you require. You're not limited by the configurations offered by manufacturers, allowing you to build a machine that truly excels in the areas that matter most to you.

- **Value:** In many cases, building your own PC can be more cost-effective than buying a pre-built one with comparable specifications. You can often find better deals on individual components, and you're not paying for the labor costs associated with assembly.

- **Learning Experience:** Building your own PC is an incredibly valuable learning experience. You'll gain a deep understanding of how computers work, which can be beneficial for troubleshooting, upgrading, and even just appreciating the technology you use every day.

- **Satisfaction:** There's a unique sense of accomplishment that comes with building something yourself. When you power on your newly built PC for the first time, you'll know that you created it with your own hands, and that feeling is hard to beat.

What You'll Learn in This Book

This book is structured to provide a comprehensive, step-by-step guide to building your own PC. We'll start with the fundamentals, covering the essential components that make up a computer and how they work together. From there, we'll delve into the specifics of choosing the right parts for your needs, considering factors like budget, performance requirements, and compatibility.

We'll cover everything from selecting the perfect processor and motherboard to understanding the intricacies of RAM, graphics cards, and storage solutions. You'll learn about power supplies, cases, and cooling systems, ensuring that your PC not only performs well but also looks great and stays cool under pressure.

Once we've covered the selection process, we'll move on to the actual assembly. Don't worry; we'll guide you through each step with clear, detailed instructions and illustrations. You'll learn how to install the motherboard, CPU, cooler, RAM, graphics card, and storage devices. We'll also cover cable management, a crucial aspect of building a clean and efficient system.

After the physical build is complete, we'll walk you through the software side of things. You'll learn how to install your operating system, drivers, and essential software. We'll also touch on basic BIOS/UEFI configuration, testing and troubleshooting, and even a brief introduction to overclocking, should you choose to explore that option.

Finally, we'll discuss peripherals, helping you choose the right keyboard, mouse, and monitor to complete your setup. We'll also cover future upgrades and maintenance, ensuring that your PC remains in top shape for years to come.

No Prior Experience Required

This book is written specifically for beginners, so you don't need any prior experience in PC building to get started. We'll explain everything in plain English, avoiding technical jargon whenever possible. We'll also provide plenty of visual aids to help you understand the concepts and procedures involved.

The only things you'll need are a willingness to learn, a bit of patience, and a few basic tools, which we'll discuss in detail in Chapter 10.

Let's Get Started!

Building your own PC is a rewarding journey, and we're excited to be your guides. By the end of this book, you'll have the knowledge and confidence to build your dream machine, tailored perfectly to your needs and preferences. So, let's dive in and start building!

CHAPTER ONE: Understanding PC Components: A Beginner's Overview

So you're ready to embark on your PC-building adventure? Excellent! Before we dive into the nitty-gritty of choosing specific parts and putting them all together, it's essential to have a basic understanding of what makes a computer tick. In this chapter, we'll take a look at the core components found in a typical desktop PC, explain their functions, and explore how they interact with each other. Think of this as a guided tour of the inner workings of your future machine. By the end of this chapter, you will be familiar with all the essential parts of a computer, and ready to move on to learning more about the specifics of each one, starting with the Central Processing Unit or CPU.

The Brain: Central Processing Unit (CPU)

The CPU, or Central Processing Unit, is often referred to as the "brain" of the computer, and for good reason. This small but mighty chip is responsible for executing instructions, performing calculations, and generally managing the flow of data throughout the system. Every click, every keystroke, every program you run – it all goes through the CPU. The CPU's performance is measured primarily by its clock speed (measured in gigahertz, or GHz) and the number of cores it has. A higher clock speed generally means faster processing, while more cores allow the CPU to handle multiple tasks simultaneously. Modern CPUs often feature hyper-threading or simultaneous multithreading (SMT), which allows a single core to act as two virtual cores, further enhancing multitasking capabilities.

It is important to note that, while a faster CPU with more cores is generally preferable, the optimal choice depends heavily on your intended use case. A basic office computer for web browsing and document editing won't need as much CPU power as a high-end gaming rig or a workstation for video editing. We'll explore the nuances of CPU selection in more detail in Chapter 2.

The Foundation: Motherboard

If the CPU is the brain, then the motherboard is the central nervous system. This large circuit board serves as the foundation for your entire build, connecting all the other components and enabling them to communicate with each other. The motherboard houses the CPU socket, RAM slots, expansion slots for graphics cards and other peripherals, storage connectors, and various ports for connecting external devices like your keyboard, mouse, and monitor.

Motherboards come in different sizes, known as form factors, with the most common being ATX, Micro-ATX, and Mini-ITX. The form factor determines the size of the motherboard, the number of expansion slots it offers, and the type of case it will fit into. Choosing the right motherboard is crucial, as it must be compatible with your chosen CPU, RAM, and other components. It is also worth noting that most modern motherboards feature integrated components such as a network interface controller (NIC) which allows you to connect your PC to a local network and/or the internet, a sound card for audio playback and recording, and USB controllers for connecting peripherals.

The Short-Term Memory: Random Access Memory (RAM)

Random Access Memory, or RAM, is the computer's short-term memory. It's where your PC stores data that it needs to access quickly, such as the operating system, running applications, and the files you're currently working on. Unlike long-term storage devices like hard drives or SSDs, RAM is volatile, meaning that its contents are erased when the computer is powered off. The amount of RAM you need depends on your usage. More RAM allows you to run more programs simultaneously and work with larger files without experiencing slowdowns. RAM speed is measured in megahertz (MHz) or gigahertz (GHz), and faster RAM can improve overall system performance, especially in memory-intensive tasks. Another important aspect of RAM is its generation, such as DDR4 or DDR5. Newer generations offer faster speeds and greater efficiency. When selecting RAM, it's important to ensure that it's compatible with your motherboard.

The Visual Powerhouse: Graphics Card (GPU)

The Graphics Processing Unit, or GPU, is responsible for rendering all the visuals you see on your screen. While some CPUs have integrated graphics, a dedicated graphics card is essential for gaming, video editing, 3D modeling, and other visually demanding tasks. Modern GPUs are incredibly powerful, featuring their own processors and dedicated memory (known as VRAM).

The performance of a graphics card is influenced by various factors, including its clock speed, the number of processing cores, and the amount and speed of its VRAM. Choosing the right graphics card depends heavily on your intended use. A high-end GPU is crucial for playing the latest games at high settings, while a more modest card might suffice for casual gaming or basic content creation. As you might expect, graphics cards can vary greatly in price, from budget-friendly options to high-end models that cost more than some entire computers.

The Long-Term Storage: Hard Disk Drives (HDDs) and Solid-State Drives (SSDs)

While RAM provides fast, temporary storage, your computer needs a place to store your operating system, applications, and files permanently. This is where long-term storage comes in, and there are two main types: Hard Disk Drives (HDDs) and Solid-State Drives (SSDs).

HDDs are the older, more traditional storage technology. They store data on spinning magnetic platters, which are read and written to by a mechanical arm. HDDs are relatively inexpensive and offer large storage capacities, making them a good choice for storing large files like movies, music, and photos. However, they are significantly slower than SSDs due to their mechanical nature.

SSDs, on the other hand, use flash memory to store data, with no moving parts. This makes them much faster, more durable, and quieter than HDDs. SSDs dramatically improve boot times, application loading speeds, and overall system responsiveness. While SSDs used to be considerably more expensive than HDDs, their prices have come down significantly in recent years, making them the preferred choice for most users.

There's also a newer type of SSD called NVMe (Non-Volatile Memory Express) SSDs. NVMe SSDs utilize a much faster interface than traditional SATA SSDs, resulting in even greater speeds. They are typically used in high-performance systems where every bit of speed matters.

The Powerhouse: Power Supply Unit (PSU)

The Power Supply Unit, or PSU, is responsible for converting the AC power from your wall outlet into the DC power that your computer's components need to operate. Choosing a reliable and efficient PSU is crucial, as it ensures that your system receives clean, stable power.

PSUs are rated by their wattage, which indicates the maximum amount of power they can deliver. It's important to choose a PSU that can provide enough power for all your components, with some headroom for future upgrades. PSUs also come with different efficiency ratings, such as 80 Plus Bronze, Silver, Gold, Platinum, and Titanium. Higher efficiency ratings mean that the PSU wastes less energy as heat, resulting in lower electricity bills and a cooler-running system.

The Enclosure: Case

The case is the enclosure that houses all your computer's components. While it might seem like a purely aesthetic choice, the case plays a crucial role in airflow, cooling, and overall system organization. Cases come in various sizes, corresponding to motherboard form factors (ATX, Micro-ATX, Mini-ITX). They also offer different features, such as the number of drive bays, fan mounts, and cable management options.

Choosing a case with good airflow is essential for keeping your components cool. Many cases come with pre-installed fans, and you can often add more to improve cooling. Cable management features, such as grommets and tie-down points, help you keep your cables organized, improving airflow and making your build look cleaner.

The Cooler: CPU Cooler and Case Fans

As your computer runs, its components generate heat. To prevent overheating, which can lead to performance issues and even component damage, it's essential to have adequate cooling. This is where CPU coolers and case fans come into play.

The CPU cooler is a specialized heatsink and fan combination that mounts directly onto the CPU to dissipate heat. There are two main types of CPU coolers: air coolers and liquid coolers. Air coolers use a heatsink with fins to draw heat away from the CPU and a fan to blow the heat away. Liquid coolers, also known as AIO (All-In-One) coolers, use a pump to circulate liquid through a closed loop, transferring heat from the CPU to a radiator, where it's dissipated by fans. Air coolers are generally more affordable, while liquid coolers often offer better cooling performance, especially for high-end CPUs.

Case fans are mounted inside the case to improve airflow. They draw cool air into the case and exhaust hot air out, helping to keep all the components cool. The number and placement of case fans can significantly impact cooling performance.

Peripherals: Keyboard, Mouse, Monitor, and More

While not technically part of the PC itself, peripherals are essential for interacting with your computer. The most important peripherals are the keyboard, mouse, and monitor.

The keyboard is your primary input device, allowing you to type text and enter commands. Keyboards come in various types, including membrane keyboards, which are typically more affordable, and mechanical keyboards, which offer a more tactile and responsive typing experience.

The mouse is another essential input device, used for navigating the operating system and interacting with applications. Like keyboards, mice come in various types, with different sensors, button configurations, and ergonomic designs.

The monitor is your primary output device, displaying the visuals generated by your graphics card. Monitors vary greatly in size, resolution, refresh rate, and panel type. The optimal monitor depends on your usage. For example, gamers often prefer monitors with high refresh rates for smoother gameplay, while content creators might prioritize color accuracy and high resolution.

Other common peripherals include speakers or headphones for audio output, printers for printing documents, and webcams for video conferencing.

Connecting It All Together

Now that you have a basic understanding of the core PC components, let's briefly touch on how they connect and interact.

The motherboard acts as the central hub, connecting all the components. The CPU is installed into a socket on the motherboard, and the RAM modules are inserted into their respective slots. The graphics card is typically installed into a PCI Express (PCIe) x16 slot, while other expansion cards, such as sound cards or network cards, can be installed into other PCIe slots.

Storage devices, such as HDDs and SSDs, are connected to the motherboard via SATA or NVMe interfaces. The power supply connects to the motherboard, providing power to the CPU, RAM, and other components. It also connects directly to the graphics card and storage devices.

The case houses all these components, and case fans are connected to the motherboard or directly to the power supply. The CPU cooler is mounted onto the CPU and connected to the motherboard to power its fan or pump.

Peripherals, such as the keyboard, mouse, and monitor, are connected to the motherboard's I/O panel, which is located on the back of the case.

With this overview of PC components, you're well on your way to understanding the inner workings of a computer. In the following chapters, we'll delve deeper into each component, exploring the various options available and helping you choose the right parts for your specific needs and budget. Get ready to build your dream machine!

CHAPTER TWO: Choosing the Right Processor (CPU) for Your Needs

Now that you have a general understanding of the major components that make up a PC, it's time to delve into the specifics, starting with the central processing unit, or CPU. As we learned in the previous chapter, the CPU is the brain of your computer, responsible for executing instructions, performing calculations, and managing the flow of data throughout the system. Choosing the right CPU is a crucial step in building your own PC, as it will significantly impact your system's overall performance and capabilities.

In this chapter, we'll explore the key factors to consider when selecting a CPU, including its core count, clock speed, cache, and integrated graphics. We'll also discuss the two major CPU manufacturers, Intel and AMD, and their respective product lines. By the end of this chapter, you'll have a solid understanding of how to choose the perfect CPU for your needs and budget.

Understanding CPU Specifications

When comparing CPUs, you'll encounter a variety of specifications that can seem daunting at first. Let's break down the most important ones:

Cores and Threads

A core is essentially a processing unit within the CPU. Early CPUs had only a single core, meaning they could only handle one task at a time. Modern CPUs, however, feature multiple cores, allowing them to process multiple tasks simultaneously. This is known as multi-threading and significantly improves performance, especially when running multiple applications or performing demanding tasks like video editing or gaming.

Many modern CPUs also feature a technology called simultaneous multi-threading (SMT), also referred to by Intel as hyper-threading. SMT allows a single physical core to act as two virtual cores, or threads. While not as effective as having additional physical cores, SMT can still provide a noticeable performance boost in multi-threaded workloads.

The number of cores and threads a CPU has is a crucial factor to consider. For basic tasks like web browsing, office work, and light gaming, a CPU with 4 cores and 8 threads is generally sufficient. For more demanding tasks like content creation, streaming, and high-end gaming, a CPU with 6, 8, or even more cores and threads is recommended. Workstation tasks, such as complex video rendering, 3D modelling, or scientific computing will require the most cores and threads to get the best performance.

Clock Speed

Clock speed, measured in gigahertz (GHz), represents the speed at which a CPU can execute instructions. A higher clock speed generally means faster processing, but it's not the only factor determining overall performance. Modern CPUs often have a base clock speed and a boost clock speed. The base clock speed is the guaranteed minimum speed the CPU will run at, while the boost clock speed is the maximum speed the CPU can reach under optimal conditions.

While clock speed is important, it's crucial to consider it in conjunction with the number of cores and threads. A CPU with a high clock speed but fewer cores might outperform a CPU with a lower clock speed but more cores in single-threaded tasks, but the latter will likely excel in multi-threaded workloads.

Cache

Cache is a small amount of very fast memory that's built directly into the CPU. It stores frequently accessed data, allowing the CPU to retrieve it much faster than if it had to access the main system RAM. CPUs typically have three levels of cache: L1, L2, and L3.

L1 cache is the smallest and fastest, followed by L2 and then L3. A larger cache generally improves performance, especially in applications that repeatedly access the same data.

Integrated Graphics

Many CPUs come with integrated graphics, meaning they have a built-in graphics processing unit (GPU). This eliminates the need for a separate, dedicated graphics card for basic display output. Integrated graphics are generally sufficient for everyday tasks like web browsing, office work, and watching videos. However, they are typically not powerful enough for gaming or other visually demanding applications.

If you plan to use your PC for gaming, video editing, or other graphics-intensive tasks, you'll likely want to invest in a dedicated graphics card. However, if you're on a tight budget or only need basic display capabilities, a CPU with integrated graphics can be a good option. It's worth noting that some CPUs, particularly those aimed at high-end workstations, do not feature integrated graphics at all.

Thermal Design Power (TDP)

Thermal Design Power, or TDP, is a measure of the maximum amount of heat a CPU is expected to generate under typical usage. It's measured in watts and is an important factor to consider when choosing a CPU cooler. A CPU with a higher TDP will require a more robust cooling solution to prevent overheating.

Socket Type

The socket type is the physical interface that connects the CPU to the motherboard. It's crucial to ensure that the CPU you choose is compatible with the socket type on your motherboard. Different CPU manufacturers and even different generations of CPUs from the same manufacturer often use different socket types. For example, Intel's 12th and 13th-generation Core processors use the LGA 1700 socket, while AMD's Ryzen 7000 series processors use the AM5 socket.

Intel vs. AMD

The two major CPU manufacturers are Intel and AMD. Both companies offer a wide range of processors for different needs and budgets. Historically, Intel has been known for its strong single-threaded performance, while AMD has often offered better multi-threaded performance at a lower price. However, the competition between the two companies is fierce, and the landscape is constantly changing.

Intel's Product Lines

Intel's consumer CPU lineup is primarily divided into the following series:

- **Core i3:** Entry-level processors, typically with 4 cores and 4 or 8 threads. Suitable for basic tasks and light gaming.

- **Core i5:** Mid-range processors, typically with 6 cores and 12 threads. A good choice for mainstream users and gamers.

- **Core i7:** High-end processors, typically with 8 or more cores and 16 or more threads. Ideal for demanding users, content creators, and high-end gamers.

- **Core i9:** Enthusiast-level processors, typically with 10 or more cores and 20 or more threads. Designed for the most demanding users and workstations.

Within each series, there are different models with varying clock speeds, cache sizes, and other features. Intel also offers unlocked processors, denoted by a "K" suffix, which can be overclocked for even greater performance.

AMD's Product Lines

AMD's consumer CPU lineup is primarily divided into the following series:

- **Ryzen 3:** Entry-level processors, typically with 4 cores and 8 threads. Suitable for basic tasks and light gaming.

- **Ryzen 5:** Mid-range processors, typically with 6 cores and 12 threads. A good choice for mainstream users and gamers.

- **Ryzen 7:** High-end processors, typically with 8 cores and 16 threads. Ideal for demanding users, content creators, and high-end gamers.

- **Ryzen 9:** Enthusiast-level processors, typically with 12 or more cores and 24 or more threads. Designed for the most demanding users and workstations.

Like Intel, AMD offers different models within each series, with varying specifications. AMD also offers unlocked processors, denoted by an "X" suffix, which can be overclocked.

Choosing the Right CPU for Your Needs

Now that you understand the key CPU specifications and the product lines offered by Intel and AMD, let's discuss how to choose the right CPU for your specific needs.

Consider Your Usage

The first and most important factor to consider is how you intend to use your PC. If you're primarily using it for basic tasks like web browsing, office work, and watching videos, an entry-level CPU with 4 cores and integrated graphics will likely suffice. If you're a gamer, you'll want to prioritize a CPU with a higher clock speed and a good balance of cores and threads, along with a dedicated graphics card. For content creation, streaming, and other multi-threaded workloads, a CPU with more cores and threads is crucial.

Set a Budget

CPUs can range in price from under $100 to over $1000. It's important to set a budget before you start shopping and stick to it.

Keep in mind that the CPU is just one component of your PC, and you'll need to allocate funds for other parts as well.

Consider Future Upgradability

While it's important to choose a CPU that meets your current needs, it's also worth considering future upgradability. If you choose a motherboard with a socket type that supports multiple generations of CPUs, you'll have more options for upgrading your processor in the future without having to replace your motherboard.

Read Reviews and Benchmarks

Once you've narrowed down your choices, it's a good idea to read reviews and look at benchmarks to see how different CPUs perform in real-world scenarios. Websites like AnandTech, Tom's Hardware, and Gamers Nexus provide in-depth reviews and benchmarks of various CPUs.

Don't Overlook the CPU Cooler

As mentioned earlier, the TDP of your chosen CPU will determine the type of cooler you need. While some CPUs come with a stock cooler included, these are often only adequate for basic usage. If you plan to overclock your CPU or run demanding applications, you'll likely want to invest in a more robust aftermarket cooler.

Making Your Decision

Choosing the right CPU can seem like a daunting task, but by understanding the key specifications, considering your usage and budget, and doing your research, you can make an informed decision that will set your PC build up for success. Remember, the CPU is the brain of your computer, so it's worth taking the time to choose the right one for your needs.

Once you have selected your CPU, you can move on to choosing the next critical component in your build, the motherboard, which will be the subject of our next chapter.

CHAPTER THREE: Motherboards: The Foundation of Your Build

With the brain of your computer, the CPU, chosen, it's time to move on to the foundation upon which your entire system will be built: the motherboard. As we briefly touched upon in Chapter 1, the motherboard is the central nervous system of your PC, connecting all the other components and enabling them to communicate and work together seamlessly. Choosing the right motherboard is just as crucial as selecting the right CPU, as it will determine the compatibility of your other components, the features available to you, and the overall stability and expandability of your system.

In this chapter, we'll take a deep dive into the world of motherboards. We'll explore the different form factors, chipsets, and features available, and we'll discuss how to choose the right motherboard for your specific needs and budget. By the end of this chapter, you'll have a solid understanding of what makes a motherboard tick and how to select the perfect one for your dream build.

Understanding Motherboard Form Factors

The first thing to consider when choosing a motherboard is its form factor. The form factor refers to the motherboard's physical size and layout, and it determines the type of case it will fit into, the number of expansion slots it offers, and the overall organization of the components. There are several form factors available, but the most common ones for consumer PCs are ATX, Micro-ATX, and Mini-ITX.

- **ATX (Advanced Technology eXtended):** ATX is the most common form factor for desktop PCs. ATX motherboards typically measure 12 × 9.6 inches (305 × 244 mm) and offer the most expansion slots, including multiple PCI Express (PCIe) slots for graphics cards and other peripherals, several RAM slots, and numerous storage connectors. ATX motherboards are a good choice for users who want maximum flexibility and expandability.

- **Micro-ATX:** Micro-ATX is a smaller version of ATX, typically measuring 9.6 × 9.6 inches (244 × 244 mm). Micro-ATX motherboards offer fewer expansion slots than ATX but are still suitable for most users. They are a good choice for users who want a smaller PC or are on a tighter budget, as Micro-ATX motherboards and cases are often more affordable.

- **Mini-ITX:** Mini-ITX is the smallest of the three common form factors, typically measuring 6.7 × 6.7 inches (170 × 170 mm). Mini-ITX motherboards offer the fewest expansion slots, usually only one PCIe slot and two RAM slots. They are designed for compact, space-saving builds, such as home theater PCs or small form factor gaming rigs.

Choosing the right form factor depends on your needs and preferences. If you want maximum expandability and flexibility, ATX is the way to go. If you want a smaller, more compact build, Micro-ATX or Mini-ITX might be a better choice. Keep in mind that the form factor of your motherboard must match the form factor of your case. An ATX motherboard won't fit into a Micro-ATX or Mini-ITX case, and vice versa.

Chipsets: The Traffic Cops of Your Motherboard

The chipset is a crucial component of the motherboard, acting as the "traffic cop" that directs the flow of data between the CPU, RAM, storage devices, and other peripherals. The chipset determines many of the features available on the motherboard, such as the number of USB ports, the type of storage interfaces supported, and whether overclocking is possible.

Both Intel and AMD offer a range of chipsets for their respective CPUs. Chipsets are typically divided into different tiers, from entry-level to high-end, with each tier offering a different set of features and capabilities.

Intel Chipsets

For Intel's 12th and 13th generation Core processors (LGA 1700 socket), the main consumer chipsets are:

- **H610:** The most basic chipset, offering limited features and no overclocking support. Suitable for budget builds.

- **B660:** A mid-range chipset that offers more features than H610, such as more USB ports and faster storage options. Supports memory overclocking but not CPU overclocking.

- **H670:** Similar to B660 but with additional PCIe lanes, making it suitable for users with multiple high-speed storage devices or expansion cards.

- **Z690/Z790:** The high-end chipsets, offering the most features and full overclocking support for both the CPU and memory. Ideal for enthusiasts and power users.

AMD Chipsets

For AMD's Ryzen 7000 series processors (AM5 socket), the main consumer chipsets are:

- **A620:** The entry-level chipset, offering basic features and limited connectivity options. Suitable for budget-conscious users.

- **B650:** A mid-range chipset that provides a good balance of features and performance. Supports memory and CPU overclocking.

- **X670:** The high-end chipset, offering the most features, including more PCIe lanes and USB ports. Supports extensive overclocking capabilities.

- **X670E:** The enthusiast-grade chipset, offering a similar feature set to X670 but with a focus on PCIe 5.0 support for next-generation graphics cards and storage devices.

When choosing a chipset, it's important to consider your needs and budget. If you're building a basic PC for everyday tasks, an entry-level chipset might suffice. If you're a gamer or content creator, a mid-range or high-end chipset will offer more features and better performance. And if you're an enthusiast who wants to push your system to its limits, a high-end chipset with overclocking support is the way to go.

Key Motherboard Features

In addition to the form factor and chipset, there are several other key features to consider when choosing a motherboard:

CPU Socket

As we discussed in Chapter 2, the CPU socket is the physical interface that connects the CPU to the motherboard. It's crucial to ensure that your motherboard has the correct socket type for your chosen CPU. For example, Intel's 12th and 13th generation Core processors use the LGA 1700 socket, while AMD's Ryzen 7000 series processors use the AM5 socket.

RAM Slots

The RAM slots are where you install your system's memory modules. Most motherboards have two or four RAM slots, although some high-end models may have eight. The number of RAM slots determines the maximum amount of RAM you can install in your system. It's also important to check the type of RAM supported by the motherboard (e.g., DDR4 or DDR5) and the maximum supported speed.

Expansion Slots

Expansion slots are used to install additional components, such as graphics cards, sound cards, network cards, and capture cards. The most common type of expansion slot is PCI Express (PCIe). PCIe slots come in different sizes (x1, x4, x8, x16) and generations (3.0, 4.0, 5.0), with each generation offering double the bandwidth of the previous one.

The number and type of PCIe slots available depend on the motherboard's form factor and chipset. ATX motherboards typically offer the most PCIe slots, while Mini-ITX motherboards usually only have one. Most modern graphics cards use a PCIe x16 slot, so make sure your motherboard has at least one of those if you plan to install a dedicated GPU.

Storage Connectors

Storage connectors are used to connect hard drives, SSDs, and optical drives to the motherboard. The most common types of storage connectors are SATA and M.2.

SATA (Serial ATA) is the older, more traditional interface for connecting storage devices. Most motherboards have several SATA ports, typically four to eight. SATA is suitable for both HDDs and SSDs, but it's limited to a maximum theoretical speed of 6 Gbps (around 550 MB/s in practice).

M.2 is a newer, faster interface that's primarily used for SSDs. M.2 slots can support both SATA and NVMe (Non-Volatile Memory Express) SSDs. NVMe SSDs are much faster than SATA SSDs, offering speeds of up to several gigabytes per second, depending on the drive and the PCIe generation supported by the M.2 slot.

The number and type of storage connectors available depend on the motherboard's chipset and form factor. Most modern motherboards have at least one or two M.2 slots and several SATA ports.

USB Ports

USB (Universal Serial Bus) ports are used to connect a wide range of peripherals, such as keyboards, mice, printers, external storage devices, and more. Motherboards typically have a variety of USB ports on the rear I/O panel and internal USB headers for connecting front panel USB ports on your case.

USB ports come in different generations (2.0, 3.0, 3.1, 3.2, 4) and types (Type-A, Type-B, Type-C), with each generation offering faster speeds and each type having a different physical connector. USB Type-C is the newest and most versatile type, as it's reversible and can be used for charging, data transfer, and video output.

The number and type of USB ports available depend on the motherboard's chipset and design. Most modern motherboards have a mix of USB 2.0, 3.0, and 3.1 ports, with some also including USB 3.2 or USB 4 ports.

Networking

Most motherboards have a built-in Ethernet port for connecting to a wired network. The speed of the Ethernet port can vary, with most modern motherboards offering Gigabit Ethernet (1 Gbps) and some higher-end models offering 2.5 Gbps or even 10 Gbps Ethernet.

Many motherboards also have built-in Wi-Fi and Bluetooth, allowing you to connect to wireless networks and devices without the need for a separate adapter. The specific Wi-Fi and Bluetooth standards supported (e.g., Wi-Fi 5, Wi-Fi 6, Wi-Fi 6E, Bluetooth 5.0, 5.1, 5.2) can vary depending on the motherboard.

Audio

Most motherboards have integrated audio, meaning they have a built-in sound card that can handle basic audio input and output. The quality of the integrated audio can vary depending on the motherboard's chipset and audio codec. Some higher-end motherboards feature more advanced audio solutions, such as dedicated audio capacitors, headphone amplifiers, and support for high-resolution audio formats.

Other Features

In addition to the core features discussed above, motherboards can offer a variety of other features, such as:

- **BIOS/UEFI:** The BIOS (Basic Input/Output System) or UEFI (Unified Extensible Firmware Interface) is the firmware that controls the motherboard's basic functions and allows you to configure various settings, such as boot order, overclocking options, and fan profiles.

- **RGB Lighting:** Many modern motherboards feature RGB lighting, which allows you to customize the look of your build with various colors and effects.

- **Fan Headers:** Fan headers are used to connect case fans and CPU coolers to the motherboard. The number and type of fan headers (3-pin or 4-pin PWM) can vary depending on the motherboard.

- **Debug LEDs/Post Code Display:** Some motherboards have debug LEDs or a post code display that can help you troubleshoot issues during the boot process.

- **Clear CMOS Button/Jumper:** A clear CMOS button or jumper allows you to reset the motherboard's BIOS settings to their defaults, which can be helpful if you encounter issues after changing settings.

Choosing the Right Motherboard for Your Needs

Now that you understand the key features and specifications of motherboards, let's discuss how to choose the right one for your specific needs:

1. Ensure CPU Compatibility

The first and most important step is to ensure that the motherboard you choose is compatible with your chosen CPU. Check the motherboard's specifications to make sure it has the correct socket type for your CPU (e.g., LGA 1700 for Intel 12th and 13th gen, AM5 for AMD Ryzen 7000 series).

2. Choose the Right Form Factor

Next, choose the right form factor for your needs and preferences. If you want maximum expandability and flexibility, go with ATX. If you want a smaller build, consider Micro-ATX or Mini-ITX. Keep in mind that your motherboard's form factor must match your case's form factor.

3. Select the Appropriate Chipset

Choose a chipset that offers the features you need. If you're building a basic PC, an entry-level chipset might suffice. If you're a gamer or content creator, a mid-range or high-end chipset will offer more features and better performance. If you plan to overclock, make sure the chipset supports it.

4. Consider Your RAM Needs

Make sure the motherboard has enough RAM slots for your needs and supports the type and speed of RAM you want to use. Most users will be fine with two or four RAM slots and DDR4 or DDR5 RAM.

5. Check the Expansion Slots

If you plan to install a dedicated graphics card, make sure the motherboard has at least one PCIe x16 slot. If you need other expansion cards, such as a sound card or network card, make sure the motherboard has enough PCIe slots of the appropriate size and generation.

6. Evaluate the Storage Options

Make sure the motherboard has enough SATA and/or M.2 slots for your storage needs. If you plan to use NVMe SSDs, make sure the M.2 slots support them and offer the desired speed (PCIe 3.0, 4.0, or 5.0).

7. Look at the USB and Networking Options

Make sure the motherboard has enough USB ports of the desired type and generation for your peripherals. If you need fast wired networking, look for a motherboard with 2.5 Gbps or 10 Gbps Ethernet. If you need wireless connectivity, make sure the motherboard has built-in Wi-Fi and Bluetooth or consider a separate adapter.

8. Consider the Audio Quality

If you're an audiophile or need high-quality audio for content creation, look for a motherboard with a good integrated audio solution or consider a dedicated sound card.

9. Read Reviews and Compare Models

Once you've narrowed down your choices based on the above criteria, it's a good idea to read reviews of specific motherboard models and compare their features, performance, and price. Websites like Tom's Hardware, AnandTech, and PCPartPicker can be valuable resources for researching and comparing motherboards.

10. Don't Forget About Aesthetics

While not as important as the technical specifications, the aesthetics of the motherboard can also be a factor for some users. If you're building a PC with a windowed case and care about the look of your build, you might want to choose a motherboard with a design and color scheme that matches your other components and overall theme. Some motherboards also feature RGB lighting, which can add a touch of customization to your build.

Conclusion

Choosing the right motherboard is a crucial step in building your own PC. By understanding the different form factors, chipsets, and features available, and by considering your specific needs and budget, you can select a motherboard that will serve as a solid foundation for your dream build. With your CPU and motherboard chosen, you're well on your way to assembling your own custom PC. In the next chapter, we'll move on to another essential component: RAM. We'll explore the different types and speeds of memory available and help you choose the right RAM for your system.

CHAPTER FOUR: All About RAM: Understanding Memory Types and Speeds

With your CPU and motherboard selected, it's time to turn our attention to another critical component of your PC build: Random Access Memory, or RAM. As we briefly discussed in Chapter 1, RAM serves as your computer's short-term memory, providing a high-speed workspace for the operating system, applications, and data that your CPU needs to access quickly. Choosing the right type and amount of RAM is essential for ensuring smooth multitasking, fast loading times, and overall system responsiveness.

In this chapter, we'll delve into the world of RAM, exploring the different types, speeds, and configurations available. We'll discuss how RAM works, what specifications to look for, and how to choose the right RAM for your specific needs and budget. By the end of this chapter, you'll have a solid understanding of RAM and be ready to make an informed decision for your PC build.

How RAM Works: A Temporary Workspace

To understand how RAM works, it's helpful to think of it as a temporary workspace for your computer. When you open a program, load a file, or browse the web, the data needed for those tasks is loaded from your long-term storage (HDD or SSD) into RAM. The CPU can then access this data much faster from RAM than it could from the storage drive, resulting in quicker loading times and smoother performance.

Unlike long-term storage, RAM is volatile, meaning that its contents are lost when the computer is powered off or restarted. This is why it's important to save your work regularly to your long-term storage, as any unsaved changes will be lost if the power goes out or the system crashes.

Types of RAM: DDR3, DDR4, and DDR5

Over the years, several types of RAM have been used in computers. The most common types in modern PCs are DDR3, DDR4, and DDR5. These acronyms stand for Double Data Rate (version number) Synchronous Dynamic Random-Access Memory. Let's break down what that means:

- **Double Data Rate (DDR):** This refers to the fact that DDR RAM can transfer data on both the rising and falling edges of the clock signal, effectively doubling the data transfer rate compared to older SDRAM (Single Data Rate) technology.

- **Synchronous:** This means that the RAM operates in sync with the system clock, allowing for more precise timing and faster data transfer.

- **Dynamic:** This refers to the way that the RAM stores data, using capacitors that need to be periodically refreshed to maintain the stored information.

- **Random-Access:** This means that the CPU can access any memory location directly, without having to read through preceding locations, allowing for fast and efficient data retrieval.

Each generation of DDR RAM offers improvements in speed, power efficiency, and capacity compared to its predecessors. Here's a brief overview of the main types:

- **DDR3:** DDR3 was the dominant RAM standard for many years, but it's now considered outdated. DDR3 RAM operates at lower speeds and higher voltages than DDR4 or DDR5, and it's not compatible with modern motherboards. If you're building a new PC, you should avoid DDR3.

- **DDR4:** DDR4 is the most common type of RAM in use today. It offers faster speeds, lower power consumption, and higher capacities than DDR3. DDR4 RAM is available in a wide range of speeds, from 2133 MT/s to over 5000

MT/s. Most modern CPUs and motherboards support DDR4.

- **DDR5:** DDR5 is the newest generation of RAM, offering even greater performance and efficiency than DDR4. DDR5 RAM starts at speeds of 4800 MT/s and can reach speeds of over 8000 MT/s. DDR5 also introduces new features, such as on-die ECC (Error Correction Code) and improved power management. However, DDR5 is currently only supported by the latest CPUs and motherboards, and it's generally more expensive than DDR4.

When choosing RAM, it's crucial to ensure that it's compatible with your motherboard. Motherboards are designed to support a specific type of RAM, and you can't mix and match different types. For example, a motherboard that supports DDR4 RAM won't work with DDR5 RAM, and vice versa.

RAM Speed and Timings: Understanding the Numbers

RAM speed is typically measured in megatransfers per second (MT/s), which represents the number of data transfers that can occur in one second. For example, DDR4-3200 RAM can perform 3.2 billion data transfers per second. Higher RAM speeds generally result in better performance, especially in memory-intensive tasks like gaming, video editing, and multitasking.

However, RAM speed isn't the only factor that affects performance. RAM timings, also known as latency, play a significant role as well. RAM timings are a series of numbers that represent the number of clock cycles required for various memory operations, such as accessing a specific column of data or switching between rows.

The most common RAM timings are:

- **CAS Latency (CL):** The number of clock cycles between sending a column address to the memory and the beginning of the data in response.

- **tRCD (RAS to CAS Delay):** The number of clock cycles between activating a row and accessing a column in that row.

- **tRP (RAS Precharge Time):** The number of clock cycles required to precharge a row before accessing a different row.

- **tRAS (Row Active Time):** The minimum number of clock cycles that a row must be active to ensure that data can be properly read or written.

Lower RAM timings generally result in better performance, as the RAM can respond more quickly to requests from the CPU. However, RAM timings are often inversely related to RAM speed. Faster RAM typically has higher timings, while slower RAM often has lower timings.

When comparing RAM modules, it's important to consider both the speed and timings. A module with a higher speed but significantly higher timings might not offer a noticeable performance improvement over a module with a lower speed but lower timings.

RAM Capacity: How Much Do You Need?

The amount of RAM you need depends on your usage patterns. More RAM allows you to run more programs simultaneously, work with larger files, and enjoy smoother multitasking without experiencing slowdowns. Here's a general guideline for RAM capacity:

- **8GB:** 8GB of RAM is the bare minimum for a modern PC. It's sufficient for basic tasks like web browsing, email, and office work, but you might experience slowdowns when running multiple programs or working with large files.

- **16GB:** 16GB of RAM is the recommended amount for most users. It provides a good balance of performance and value, allowing for smooth multitasking, gaming, and light content creation.

- **32GB:** 32GB of RAM is ideal for power users, gamers, and content creators who work with demanding applications, large files, or multiple virtual machines.

- **64GB and beyond:** 64GB or more of RAM is typically only necessary for specialized workstations and servers that handle extremely demanding workloads, such as high-resolution video editing, 3D rendering, and scientific simulations.

It's important to note that having more RAM than you need won't necessarily improve performance. Once you have enough RAM to handle your typical workloads, adding more won't make your computer faster. However, having too little RAM can significantly impact performance, causing your system to slow down and become unresponsive as it relies on slower storage as virtual memory.

RAM Configuration: Single-Channel vs. Dual-Channel vs. Quad-Channel

RAM modules can be installed in different configurations, which can affect performance. The most common configurations are single-channel, dual-channel, and quad-channel.

- **Single-channel:** In a single-channel configuration, the CPU communicates with the RAM through a single 64-bit channel. This is the simplest configuration, but it offers the lowest bandwidth and performance.

- **Dual-channel:** In a dual-channel configuration, the CPU communicates with the RAM through two 64-bit channels, effectively doubling the bandwidth compared to single-channel. This results in improved performance, especially in memory-intensive tasks. Most modern motherboards support dual-channel RAM. To enable dual-channel mode, you need to install two identical RAM modules in the correct slots, which are usually color-coded.

- **Quad-channel:** In a quad-channel configuration, the CPU communicates with the RAM through four 64-bit channels, quadrupling the bandwidth compared to single-channel. This offers the highest performance but is typically only supported by high-end desktop (HEDT) and server platforms.

For most users, a dual-channel configuration offers the best balance of performance and value. It's important to check your motherboard's manual to determine the correct slots for enabling dual-channel mode.

RAM Kits vs. Single Modules: What's the Difference?

RAM is typically sold as either single modules or kits of two or more modules. While you can technically mix and match RAM modules from different manufacturers or with different specifications, it's generally not recommended.

RAM kits are tested and guaranteed to work together at their rated speed and timings. When you buy a kit, you can be confident that the modules will be compatible and offer optimal performance in a dual-channel or quad-channel configuration.

Mixing and matching RAM modules can lead to compatibility issues, instability, or reduced performance. If you do decide to mix modules, it's important to ensure that they have the same specifications (type, speed, timings, voltage) and install them in the correct slots for your desired configuration.

Overclocking RAM: Pushing the Limits

Like CPUs, RAM can also be overclocked to run at speeds beyond its official rating. Overclocking RAM can improve performance in memory-intensive tasks, but it also comes with some risks.

Overclocking RAM involves increasing its clock speed, adjusting its timings, and sometimes increasing its voltage. This can generate more heat and potentially reduce the lifespan of the modules if not done carefully.

Most modern motherboards offer RAM overclocking options in the BIOS/UEFI. However, not all RAM modules are equally good at overclocking. Some modules are specifically designed and binned for overclocking, while others might not be able to handle much beyond their rated speeds.

If you decide to overclock your RAM, it's important to do so gradually, testing for stability at each step. You should also monitor the RAM temperature and ensure that it has adequate cooling.

XMP and DOCP: Easy RAM Overclocking

To simplify RAM overclocking, many RAM modules support a feature called XMP (Extreme Memory Profile) or DOCP (Direct Over Clock Profile). XMP is an Intel technology, while DOCP is an AMD technology, but they both serve the same purpose.

XMP/DOCP profiles are pre-defined overclocking settings that are stored on the RAM modules themselves. When you enable XMP/DOCP in the BIOS/UEFI, the motherboard automatically applies these settings, allowing the RAM to run at its rated overclocked speed and timings without manual configuration.

Most modern RAM kits come with one or more XMP/DOCP profiles. Enabling XMP/DOCP is a simple and safe way to get the most performance out of your RAM, as long as your motherboard supports it.

ECC RAM: Error Correction for Critical Systems

ECC (Error Correction Code) RAM is a type of memory that can detect and correct certain types of memory errors. ECC RAM is primarily used in servers and workstations where data integrity is critical, such as financial institutions, scientific research, and medical imaging.

ECC RAM has an extra chip that adds a parity bit to each byte of data. This allows the RAM to detect and correct single-bit errors, where a single bit of data is flipped from 0 to 1 or vice versa. Some ECC RAM can also detect multi-bit errors, although it can't correct them.

ECC RAM is typically more expensive than non-ECC RAM and requires a motherboard and CPU that support it. For most consumer PCs, ECC RAM is not necessary.

Choosing the Right RAM for Your Build

Now that you understand the key features and specifications of RAM, let's discuss how to choose the right RAM for your specific needs:

1. **Determine Compatibility:** The first step is to ensure that the RAM you choose is compatible with your motherboard. Check your motherboard's specifications to determine the type of RAM it supports (DDR4 or DDR5), the maximum supported speed, and the maximum capacity.

2. **Choose the Right Capacity:** Next, choose the right capacity for your needs. 8GB is the bare minimum for a modern PC, 16GB is recommended for most users, 32GB is ideal for power users and content creators, and 64GB or more is typically only necessary for specialized workstations and servers.

3. **Consider Speed and Timings:** Look for RAM with a good balance of speed and timings. Higher speeds generally offer better performance, but timings also play a

significant role. For most users, DDR4-3200 or DDR4-3600 with CL16 or CL18 timings offers a good balance of performance and value. For DDR5, look for speeds of 5200 MT/s or higher with CL38 or lower timings.

4. **Choose a Reputable Brand:** Stick with reputable RAM brands that have a good track record for quality and reliability. Some popular and well-regarded RAM brands include Corsair, G.Skill, Crucial, Kingston, and Team Group.

5. **Decide on a Kit or Single Modules:** If you're building a new PC, it's generally recommended to buy a RAM kit rather than mixing and matching single modules. Kits are tested and guaranteed to work together, ensuring optimal performance and stability.

6. **Consider Overclocking:** If you're interested in overclocking, look for RAM that's specifically designed for it or has good reviews for overclocking potential. Also, make sure your motherboard supports RAM overclocking and consider enabling XMP/DOCP for easy overclocking.

7. **Think About Aesthetics:** While not as important as performance, the aesthetics of the RAM can also be a factor for some users. Many RAM modules come with heat spreaders in various colors and designs, and some even feature RGB lighting. If you're building a PC with a windowed case and care about the look of your build, you might want to choose RAM that matches your other components and overall theme.

RAM Type	Typical Speed Range	Typical CAS Latency	Recommended Use Case
DDR3	800 - 2133 MT/s	9 - 11	Outdated, not recommended for new builds
DDR4	2133 - 5000+ MT/s	14 - 20	Mainstream users, gamers, content creators

| DDR5 | 4800 - 8000+ MT/s | 30 - 40 | Enthusiasts, high-end gaming, demanding workloads |

Installing RAM: A Simple Process

Installing RAM is a relatively simple process, but it's important to do it correctly to avoid damaging the modules or the motherboard. Here's a step-by-step guide:

1. **Power Off and Unplug:** Before installing RAM, make sure your computer is powered off and unplugged from the wall outlet.

2. **Ground Yourself:** To prevent electrostatic discharge (ESD), which can damage electronic components, it's important to ground yourself before handling RAM. You can do this by touching a grounded metal object, such as the computer case, or by wearing an anti-static wrist strap.

3. **Open the Case:** Open your computer case and locate the RAM slots on the motherboard. They are usually located near the CPU socket and are often color-coded.

4. **Release the Clips:** Each RAM slot has two clips on either end that hold the module in place. Gently push these clips outward to release them.

5. **Align the Notch:** RAM modules have a notch on the bottom that aligns with a corresponding key in the slot. Make sure the notch on the module is aligned with the key in the slot before inserting it.

6. **Insert the Module:** Holding the RAM module by the edges, gently insert it into the slot at a slight angle. Apply even pressure to both ends of the module until it clicks into place. The clips should automatically snap back into the locked position.

7. **Repeat for Other Modules:** If you're installing multiple RAM modules, repeat steps 4-6 for each module. Make sure to install them in the correct slots for your desired configuration (e.g., dual-channel).

8. **Close the Case:** Once all the RAM modules are installed, close your computer case.

9. **Power On and Check:** Reconnect the power cable, power on your computer, and enter the BIOS/UEFI to verify that the RAM is detected and running at the correct speed and timings. You can also check the RAM configuration in your operating system.

RAM is a critical component of any PC build, providing the high-speed workspace that your CPU needs to perform at its best. By understanding the different types, speeds, and configurations of RAM, and by considering your specific needs and budget, you can choose the right RAM for your system and ensure smooth multitasking, fast loading times, and overall system responsiveness. With your CPU, motherboard, and RAM selected, you're well on your way to completing your PC build. In the next chapter, we'll move on to another essential component: the graphics card.

CHAPTER FIVE: Graphics Cards (GPU): A Deep Dive for Visual Performance

Your computer's central processing unit (CPU) is a powerful workhorse, capable of handling a wide range of tasks. However, when it comes to visually demanding applications like gaming, video editing, and 3D modeling, the CPU needs a specialized helper: the Graphics Processing Unit, or GPU. Often referred to as a graphics card, the GPU is a dedicated processor that takes over the responsibility of rendering all the visuals you see on your screen, from the smooth animations in your operating system to the immersive worlds of your favorite games.

In this chapter, we'll embark on a deep dive into the realm of graphics cards. We'll explore how GPUs work, what specifications to look for, and how to choose the right one for your needs and budget. By the time we're done, you'll have a solid grasp of graphics card technology and be well-equipped to make an informed decision for your PC build.

The Role of the GPU: Bringing Pixels to Life

While the CPU is a general-purpose processor, the GPU is specifically designed to handle the complex calculations required for rendering images, videos, and 3D graphics. It accomplishes this through a massively parallel architecture, featuring thousands of smaller cores that work together to process vast amounts of data simultaneously.

Think of it like this: the CPU is like a highly skilled craftsman who can build anything, but the GPU is like a specialized factory with thousands of workers, each dedicated to a specific task in the assembly line. When it comes to rendering graphics, the GPU's parallel processing power far surpasses that of the CPU.

Here's a simplified breakdown of how the GPU works:

1. **Data Input:** The CPU sends instructions and data to the GPU, including information about the objects to be rendered, their textures, and their position in the 3D space.

2. **Vertex Processing:** The GPU's vertex shaders process the vertices of each object, transforming them from 3D coordinates into 2D coordinates that can be displayed on the screen.

3. **Rasterization:** The GPU then rasterizes the objects, converting them into a grid of pixels.

4. **Pixel Processing:** The GPU's pixel shaders apply various effects to each pixel, such as lighting, shadows, and reflections, based on the textures and materials assigned to the objects.

5. **Frame Buffering:** The processed pixels are stored in a frame buffer, which is a portion of the GPU's memory dedicated to holding the image that will be displayed on the screen.

6. **Output:** The GPU sends the contents of the frame buffer to the display, resulting in the image you see on your monitor.

This process is repeated many times per second, creating the illusion of smooth motion in games and animations. The faster the GPU can perform these steps, the higher the frame rate (measured in frames per second, or FPS) and the smoother the visuals.

Integrated vs. Dedicated Graphics: Two Paths to Visuals

There are two main types of graphics solutions: integrated and dedicated.

- **Integrated Graphics:** As we touched upon in Chapter 2, some CPUs come with integrated graphics, meaning they have a built-in GPU. Integrated graphics are typically less powerful than dedicated graphics cards, but they are sufficient for basic tasks like web browsing, office work, and watching videos. Integrated graphics share system memory (RAM) with the CPU, which can impact overall system performance.

- **Dedicated Graphics Cards:** Dedicated graphics cards are separate components that plug into a PCI Express (PCIe) x16 slot on the motherboard. They have their own dedicated memory (VRAM) and are much more powerful than integrated graphics. Dedicated graphics cards are essential for gaming, video editing, 3D modeling, and other visually demanding applications.

If you're building a PC primarily for gaming or other graphics-intensive tasks, a dedicated graphics card is a must-have. However, if you're on a tight budget or only need basic display capabilities, a CPU with integrated graphics can be a viable option, allowing you to add a dedicated graphics card later if needed.

Key Graphics Card Specifications: Understanding the Jargon

When comparing graphics cards, you'll encounter a variety of specifications that can seem overwhelming at first. Let's break down the most important ones:

GPU Cores: The Building Blocks of Performance

The number of GPU cores, sometimes referred to as CUDA cores (NVIDIA) or stream processors (AMD), is a key indicator of a graphics card's processing power. More cores generally mean better performance, as they allow the GPU to handle more calculations simultaneously. However, it's important to note that core counts are not directly comparable between different GPU architectures or manufacturers.

Clock Speed: The Pace of Processing

Clock speed, measured in megahertz (MHz) or gigahertz (GHz), represents the speed at which the GPU cores operate. A higher clock speed generally means faster processing, but like core counts, it's not the only factor determining overall performance.

Modern graphics cards often have a base clock speed and a boost clock speed. The base clock speed is the guaranteed minimum speed the GPU will run at, while the boost clock speed is the maximum speed the GPU can reach under optimal conditions, such as when there's sufficient power and cooling.

Video Memory (VRAM): The Frame Buffer's Capacity

Video memory, or VRAM, is the dedicated memory that the GPU uses to store the data it needs to render images, such as textures, models, and the frame buffer. The amount and speed of VRAM can significantly impact performance, especially at higher resolutions and with more complex graphics settings.

VRAM capacity is measured in gigabytes (GB), with modern graphics cards typically offering between 4GB and 24GB or more. More VRAM allows the GPU to store more data, reducing the need to access slower system memory and resulting in smoother performance.

VRAM speed is measured in gigabits per second (Gbps) or gigatransfers per second (GT/s) and represents the rate at which data can be transferred between the GPU and the VRAM. Faster VRAM can improve performance, especially in memory-intensive tasks.

The type of VRAM used can also impact performance. The most common types in modern graphics cards are GDDR6 and GDDR6X, with GDDR6X offering higher bandwidth than GDDR6. Some high-end cards use a more advanced type of memory called HBM2 (High Bandwidth Memory 2), which offers even greater bandwidth but is typically more expensive.

Bus Interface: The Highway to the Motherboard

The bus interface is the connection between the graphics card and the motherboard. Most modern graphics cards use the PCI Express (PCIe) x16 interface, which provides high bandwidth for data transfer.

PCIe comes in different generations, with each generation offering double the bandwidth of the previous one. The most common generations in use today are PCIe 3.0 and PCIe 4.0, with PCIe 5.0 starting to appear in high-end platforms.

While newer PCIe generations offer greater bandwidth, the actual performance impact of the bus interface is often minimal for current-generation graphics cards. Most modern GPUs don't fully saturate the bandwidth provided by PCIe 3.0, so upgrading to a PCIe 4.0 or 5.0 motherboard solely for the faster bus interface is usually not necessary.

TDP and Power Connectors: Fueling the Beast

Thermal Design Power (TDP), measured in watts, represents the maximum amount of heat a graphics card is expected to generate under typical usage. It's an important factor to consider when choosing a power supply, as you need to ensure that your PSU can provide enough power for the graphics card and other components.

Graphics cards with higher TDPs typically require additional power connectors beyond what the PCIe slot can provide. These connectors come in 6-pin and 8-pin configurations, with some high-end cards requiring two or more 8-pin connectors.

It's crucial to choose a power supply that has the necessary connectors for your chosen graphics card. Using adapters to convert 6-pin connectors to 8-pin connectors is generally not recommended, as it can lead to instability or damage to the graphics card.

Display Outputs: Connecting to Your Monitor

Graphics cards have various display outputs for connecting to monitors. The most common types are:

- **HDMI (High-Definition Multimedia Interface):** A digital interface that can transmit both video and audio signals. HDMI is commonly used for connecting to TVs and monitors.

- **DisplayPort:** A digital interface that offers higher bandwidth than HDMI, making it suitable for high-resolution and high-refresh-rate displays. DisplayPort is often preferred by gamers and professionals.

- **DVI (Digital Visual Interface):** An older digital interface that's gradually being phased out. DVI is still found on some older monitors and graphics cards.

The number and type of display outputs can vary between graphics cards. Most modern cards have at least one HDMI port and one or more DisplayPort outputs. Some cards also include a USB-C port, which can be used for video output, data transfer, and charging.

When choosing a graphics card, make sure it has the necessary display outputs for your monitor(s). If you plan to use multiple displays, make sure the card supports the desired configuration.

NVIDIA vs. AMD: The Two Titans of Graphics

The two major graphics card manufacturers are NVIDIA and AMD. Both companies offer a wide range of GPUs for different needs and budgets, from entry-level cards for basic gaming to high-end models for enthusiasts and professionals.

NVIDIA's GeForce Lineup

NVIDIA's consumer graphics card lineup is primarily branded under the GeForce name. The current generation is the GeForce RTX 40 series, which includes models like the RTX 4060, RTX 4070, RTX 4080, and RTX 4090. The previous generation was the GeForce RTX 30 series, which included models like the RTX 3060, RTX 3070, RTX 3080, and RTX 3090.

NVIDIA's graphics cards are generally known for their strong performance, particularly in high-end gaming and ray tracing. Ray tracing is a rendering technique that simulates the physical behavior of light, resulting in more realistic lighting, shadows, and reflections. NVIDIA's RTX series cards feature dedicated hardware for ray tracing acceleration, called RT cores.

NVIDIA also offers a technology called DLSS (Deep Learning Super Sampling), which uses AI to upscale lower-resolution images to higher resolutions, improving performance without a significant loss in image quality. DLSS can be particularly beneficial for gaming at high resolutions or with ray tracing enabled.

AMD's Radeon Lineup

AMD's consumer graphics card lineup is branded under the Radeon name. The current generation is the Radeon RX 7000 series, which includes models like the RX 7600, RX 7700 XT, RX 7800 XT, and RX 7900 XTX. The previous generation was the Radeon RX 6000 series, which included models like the RX 6600, RX 6700 XT, RX 6800 XT, and RX 6900 XT.

AMD's graphics cards are often praised for their strong performance-per-dollar ratio, particularly in the mid-range and high-end segments. AMD also supports ray tracing on its RX 6000 and RX 7000 series cards, although its ray tracing performance is generally not as strong as NVIDIA's.

AMD offers a technology called FSR (FidelityFX Super Resolution), which is similar to NVIDIA's DLSS in that it upscales lower-resolution images to higher resolutions to improve performance. However, FSR uses a different algorithm than DLSS and doesn't rely on dedicated AI hardware, making it compatible with a wider range of graphics cards, including older AMD models and even some NVIDIA cards.

Choosing the Right Graphics Card for Your Needs

Now that you understand the key graphics card specifications and the product lines offered by NVIDIA and AMD, let's discuss how to choose the right GPU for your specific needs:

1. Determine Your Budget

Graphics cards can range in price from under $200 to over $2000. It's important to set a budget before you start shopping and stick to it. Keep in mind that the graphics card is just one component of your PC, and you'll need to allocate funds for other parts as well.

2. Consider Your Target Resolution and Refresh Rate

The resolution and refresh rate of your monitor(s) will significantly impact your choice of graphics card. If you're gaming at 1080p and 60Hz, a mid-range card like the NVIDIA GeForce RTX 3060 or AMD Radeon RX 6600 XT should be sufficient. If you're targeting 1440p at 144Hz or higher, you'll want a more powerful card like the RTX 4070 or RX 7700 XT. And if you're aiming for 4K gaming at 60Hz or higher, you'll need a high-end card like the RTX 4080 or RX 7900 XTX.

3. Think About the Games or Applications You'll Be Using

Different games and applications have different graphics requirements. If you primarily play older or less demanding games, you might be able to get away with a less powerful graphics card. However, if you want to play the latest AAA titles at high settings, you'll need a more powerful GPU.

Similarly, if you're using your PC for professional applications like video editing or 3D modeling, you'll want to choose a graphics card that's well-suited for those tasks. Some applications are optimized for specific GPU architectures or features, so it's worth doing some research to see which cards offer the best performance for your specific use case.

4. Look at Benchmarks and Reviews

Once you've narrowed down your choices based on your budget, target resolution, and usage, it's a good idea to look at benchmarks and reviews to see how different graphics cards perform in real-world scenarios. Websites like Tom's Hardware, AnandTech, and Gamers Nexus provide in-depth reviews and benchmarks of various GPUs, covering gaming performance, power consumption, temperatures, and noise levels.

5. Consider Future-Proofing

While it's impossible to predict the future, it's worth considering how long you expect your graphics card to last before you need to upgrade. If you want your card to be able to handle the latest games at high settings for several years, you might want to invest in a more powerful model than you need for your current setup. However, keep in mind that graphics card technology advances rapidly, and today's high-end card will eventually become mid-range or even low-end over time.

6. Don't Forget About the Power Supply and Case

As mentioned earlier, it's crucial to choose a power supply that can provide enough power for your chosen graphics card and has the necessary connectors. You should also make sure that your case has enough space to accommodate the length and thickness of the card, as some high-end models can be quite large.

7. Think About Cooling and Noise

Graphics cards generate heat, especially under heavy load. Most cards come with their own cooling solutions, typically consisting of a heatsink and one or more fans. Some cards have more effective coolers than others, which can impact performance, noise levels, and overclocking potential.

If you're building a PC with a focus on quiet operation, you might want to choose a graphics card with a well-regarded cooler or consider a model with a hybrid or liquid cooling solution. However, keep in mind that these options can be more expensive and may require additional space in your case.

Graphics Card	Target Resolution	Typical VRAM	Key Features
NVIDIA GeForce RTX 3060	1080p - 1440p	12 GB GDDR6	DLSS, Ray Tracing
AMD Radeon RX 6600 XT	1080p - 1440p	8 GB GDDR6	FSR, Smart Access Memory

NVIDIA GeForce RTX 4070	1440p - 4K	12 GB GDDR6X	DLSS 3, Ray Tracing
AMD Radeon RX 7700 XT	1440p - 4K	12 GB GDDR6	FSR, Ray Tracing
NVIDIA GeForce RTX 4080	4K	16 GB GDDR6X	DLSS 3, Ray Tracing
AMD Radeon RX 7900 XTX	4K	24 GB GDDR6	FSR, Ray Tracing

Installing a Graphics Card: A Straightforward Process

Installing a graphics card is a relatively simple process, but it's important to do it correctly to avoid damaging the card or the motherboard. Here's a step-by-step guide:

- **Power Off and Unplug:** Before installing a graphics card, make sure your computer is powered off and unplugged from the wall outlet.

- **Ground Yourself:** To prevent electrostatic discharge (ESD), which can damage electronic components, it's important to ground yourself before handling a graphics card. You can do this by touching a grounded metal object, such as the computer case, or by wearing an anti-static wrist strap.

- **Open the Case:** Open your computer case and locate the PCIe x16 slot on the motherboard. It's usually the longest slot and is often located near the CPU.

- **Remove Expansion Slot Covers:** Depending on the size of your graphics card, you may need to remove one or more expansion slot covers from the back of your case. These are usually held in place by screws or clips.

- **Insert the Graphics Card:** Holding the graphics card by the edges, align it with the PCIe x16 slot and gently insert it. Apply even pressure until the card is fully seated in the slot. You should hear a click when the card is properly installed.

- **Secure the Card:** Most graphics cards have a bracket that needs to be secured to the case using one or more screws. This helps to support the weight of the card and prevent it from sagging.

- **Connect Power Cables:** If your graphics card requires additional power connectors, connect the appropriate cables from your power supply to the connectors on the card. Make sure the connectors are fully inserted and secure.

- **Close the Case:** Once the graphics card is installed and secured, close your computer case.

- **Connect the Monitor:** Connect your monitor(s) to the display output(s) on the graphics card.

- **Power On and Install Drivers:** Reconnect the power cable, power on your computer, and install the latest drivers for your graphics card. You can usually download the drivers from the NVIDIA or AMD website.

With your graphics card installed and the drivers set up, you're ready to enjoy the enhanced visual performance it offers. Whether you're gaming, creating content, or simply enjoying a more responsive and visually appealing computing experience, your GPU is a crucial component that brings your pixels to life. In the next chapter, we'll shift our focus to long-term storage solutions, exploring the differences between HDDs, SSDs, and NVMe drives.

CHAPTER SIX: Storage Solutions: HDD vs. SSD vs. NVMe

Now that we've covered the core components of your PC build – the CPU, motherboard, RAM, and graphics card – it's time to turn our attention to where you'll store your operating system, applications, and all your precious data: the storage drives. Choosing the right storage solution is crucial for ensuring fast boot times, quick application loading, and a responsive overall computing experience.

In this chapter, we'll explore the three main types of storage drives used in modern PCs: Hard Disk Drives (HDDs), Solid-State Drives (SSDs), and NVMe SSDs. We'll delve into how each type of drive works, their pros and cons, and the key specifications to consider when making your selection. By the end of this chapter, you'll have a solid understanding of the different storage options available and be ready to choose the right one (or more) for your needs and budget.

Hard Disk Drives (HDDs): The Traditional Workhorses

Hard Disk Drives, or HDDs, have been the standard for long-term storage in computers for decades. They are mechanical drives that store data on spinning magnetic platters, which are read from and written to by a moving actuator arm with a magnetic head. Think of it like a record player, but instead of a needle reading grooves on a vinyl record, the HDD's head reads and writes magnetic patterns on the platters.

How HDDs Work: A Mechanical Ballet

Here's a simplified breakdown of how an HDD operates:

1. **Platters:** The heart of an HDD is a stack of one or more rigid, circular platters coated with a thin layer of magnetic

material. These platters spin at high speeds, typically 5400 or 7200 revolutions per minute (RPM).

2. **Actuator Arm and Head:** An actuator arm, similar to the tone arm on a record player, moves across the surface of each platter. At the end of the arm is a tiny magnetic head that reads and writes data by changing the magnetic orientation of tiny areas on the platter's surface.

3. **Read/Write Operations:** To read data, the head detects the magnetic patterns on the platter as it spins. To write data, the head creates new magnetic patterns, effectively storing information as a series of 1s and 0s.

4. **Spindle Motor:** A spindle motor rotates the platters at a constant speed, allowing the head to access any part of the platter's surface.

5. **Controller:** An electronic controller manages the movement of the actuator arm, the spinning of the platters, and the flow of data between the drive and the computer.

Advantages of HDDs: Capacity and Cost

The main advantages of HDDs are their high storage capacity and relatively low cost per gigabyte. As of this writing, HDDs are available in capacities of up to 20TB or more, making them ideal for storing large amounts of data, such as photos, videos, music libraries, and game installations.

HDDs are also significantly cheaper than SSDs, especially at higher capacities. This makes them an attractive option for users on a budget or those who need to store vast amounts of data without breaking the bank.

Disadvantages of HDDs: Speed and Durability

The primary drawback of HDDs is their relatively slow speed compared to SSDs. Because HDDs rely on mechanical parts, they are limited by the physical movement of the actuator arm and the spinning of the platters. This results in slower boot times, longer application loading times, and a less responsive overall system.

HDDs are also more susceptible to damage from physical shock or vibration due to their moving parts. Dropping an HDD or subjecting it to strong vibrations can cause the head to crash into the platter's surface, potentially resulting in data loss or drive failure.

Key HDD Specifications: What to Look For

When choosing an HDD, there are several key specifications to consider:

- **Capacity:** The amount of data the drive can store, measured in gigabytes (GB) or terabytes (TB). Choose a capacity that meets your current and anticipated future needs.

- **Rotational Speed:** The speed at which the platters spin, measured in revolutions per minute (RPM). Common speeds are 5400 RPM and 7200 RPM. Higher rotational speeds generally result in faster performance but can also produce more noise and heat.

- **Cache:** A small amount of fast memory built into the drive that stores frequently accessed data, improving performance. Common cache sizes range from 64MB to 256MB or more.

- **Interface:** The connection between the drive and the motherboard. Most modern HDDs use the SATA (Serial ATA) interface, with SATA III being the most common, offering a maximum theoretical speed of 6 Gbps.

- **Form Factor:** The physical size and shape of the drive. The most common form factors for desktop HDDs are 3.5-inch and 2.5-inch. 3.5-inch drives are typically used in desktop PCs, while 2.5-inch drives are often used in laptops but can also be used in desktops with an adapter.

Solid-State Drives (SSDs): The Speed Demons

Solid-State Drives, or SSDs, have revolutionized the storage landscape in recent years. Unlike HDDs, SSDs have no moving parts. Instead, they store data on interconnected flash memory chips, similar to the technology used in USB flash drives but much faster and more sophisticated.

How SSDs Work: A Flash of Brilliance

Here's a simplified overview of how an SSD operates:

- **NAND Flash Memory:** The core of an SSD is its NAND flash memory, which is a type of non-volatile memory that retains data even when power is lost. NAND flash is organized into blocks and pages, with data being written to pages and erased in blocks.

- **Controller:** An SSD controller manages the flow of data between the flash memory and the computer. It performs various tasks, such as wear leveling, error correction, and garbage collection, to ensure the drive's performance and longevity.

- **DRAM Cache (Optional):** Many SSDs include a small amount of DRAM (Dynamic Random-Access Memory) that serves as a high-speed cache, storing frequently accessed data and improving performance. However, some entry-level SSDs are DRAM-less and rely on a portion of the NAND flash for caching or use a technology called Host Memory Buffer (HMB) to borrow a small amount of system RAM for caching.

- **Interface:** SSDs connect to the motherboard via various interfaces, with the most common being SATA and NVMe (which we'll discuss in the next section).

Advantages of SSDs: Speed, Durability, and Silence

The most significant advantage of SSDs is their speed. Because they have no moving parts, SSDs can access data much faster than HDDs, resulting in dramatically faster boot times, application loading times, and file transfer speeds. An SSD can make your entire system feel much more responsive and snappy.

SSDs are also more durable than HDDs, as they are not susceptible to damage from physical shock or vibration. This makes them a better choice for laptops or PCs that are frequently moved around.

Additionally, SSDs are silent in operation, as they have no spinning platters or moving actuator arms. This can contribute to a quieter overall computing experience.

Disadvantages of SSDs: Cost and Capacity

The main drawbacks of SSDs are their higher cost per gigabyte compared to HDDs and their generally lower maximum capacities. While SSD prices have come down significantly in recent years, they are still more expensive than HDDs, especially at higher capacities.

While SSDs are available in capacities of up to 8TB or more, these high-capacity models are typically very expensive. For most users, SSDs in the 500GB to 2TB range offer the best balance of price, performance, and capacity.

Key SSD Specifications: What to Look For

When choosing an SSD, there are several key specifications to consider:

- **Capacity:** The amount of data the drive can store, measured in gigabytes (GB) or terabytes (TB). Choose a capacity that meets your needs, keeping in mind that your operating system and applications will take up a significant portion of the drive's space.

- **Interface:** The connection between the drive and the motherboard. The two main interfaces for consumer SSDs are SATA and NVMe. SATA SSDs are limited to a maximum theoretical speed of around 550 MB/s, while NVMe SSDs can reach speeds of several gigabytes per second.

- **Form Factor:** The physical size and shape of the drive. SATA SSDs typically come in a 2.5-inch form factor, while NVMe SSDs usually use the M.2 form factor.

- **NAND Type:** The type of NAND flash memory used in the drive. The most common types are SLC (Single-Level Cell), MLC (Multi-Level Cell), TLC (Triple-Level Cell), and QLC (Quad-Level Cell). SLC is the fastest and most durable but also the most expensive. MLC offers a good balance of performance, endurance, and cost. TLC is the most common type in consumer SSDs, offering decent performance and endurance at a lower cost than MLC. QLC is the least expensive but also has the lowest performance and endurance.

- **Controller:** The SSD controller plays a crucial role in the drive's performance and features. Different controllers offer varying levels of performance, power efficiency, and support for features like encryption and error correction.

- **DRAM Cache:** As mentioned earlier, many SSDs include a DRAM cache to improve performance. However, some entry-level SSDs are DRAM-less and rely on other caching mechanisms.

- **Endurance:** SSDs have a limited lifespan in terms of the amount of data that can be written to them before they start to wear out. Endurance is typically measured in terabytes written (TBW) or drive writes per day (DWPD). Higher endurance ratings are better, especially for users who frequently write large amounts of data to their drives.

NVMe SSDs: The Performance Kings

NVMe (Non-Volatile Memory Express) SSDs represent the cutting edge of consumer storage technology. They use the NVMe interface, which is specifically designed for high-speed, non-volatile storage like flash memory. NVMe SSDs connect to the motherboard via the PCI Express (PCIe) bus, which offers much higher bandwidth than the older SATA interface.

How NVMe SSDs Work: A Direct Line to the CPU

Unlike SATA SSDs, which use a controller designed for slower, mechanical HDDs, NVMe SSDs communicate directly with the CPU via the PCIe bus. This eliminates much of the overhead and latency associated with the older SATA interface, resulting in significantly faster performance.

Advantages of NVMe SSDs: Unrivaled Speed

The primary advantage of NVMe SSDs is their speed. They can achieve sequential read and write speeds of several gigabytes per second, far surpassing the capabilities of SATA SSDs. This translates to even faster boot times, application loading times, and file transfers.

NVMe SSDs also excel in random read and write operations, which are crucial for overall system responsiveness. They can handle a much higher number of input/output operations per second (IOPS) than SATA SSDs, making them ideal for demanding workloads like gaming, content creation, and database management.

Disadvantages of NVMe SSDs: Cost and Compatibility

The main drawbacks of NVMe SSDs are their higher cost compared to SATA SSDs and their compatibility requirements. While NVMe SSD prices have come down in recent years, they are still generally more expensive than SATA SSDs of the same capacity.

To use an NVMe SSD, your motherboard must have an M.2 slot that supports the NVMe interface. Most modern motherboards have at least one M.2 slot that supports NVMe, but it's important to check your motherboard's specifications to be sure.

Additionally, some older operating systems may not have native support for NVMe drives, requiring you to install a separate driver during the OS installation process.

Key NVMe SSD Specifications: What to Look For

When choosing an NVMe SSD, many of the same specifications apply as with SATA SSDs, such as capacity, NAND type, controller, and endurance. However, there are a few additional factors to consider:

- **PCIe Generation:** NVMe SSDs use the PCIe interface, which comes in different generations (3.0, 4.0, 5.0). Each generation offers double the bandwidth of the previous one. PCIe 3.0 x4 SSDs can reach speeds of up to around 3500 MB/s, while PCIe 4.0 x4 SSDs can reach speeds of up to around 7000 MB/s, and PCIe 5.0 x4 drives can reach speeds of up to around 14,000 MB/s. To take full advantage of a PCIe 4.0 or 5.0 SSD, your motherboard and CPU must support the corresponding PCIe generation.

- **Form Factor:** Most NVMe SSDs use the M.2 form factor, which is a small, rectangular card that plugs directly into an M.2 slot on the motherboard. The most common M.2 size for NVMe SSDs is 2280, which means the card is 22mm wide and 80mm long. However, other sizes like 2242 and 22110 are also available. Make sure your motherboard has an M.2 slot that supports the size of the SSD you choose.

- **Heat Management:** Because NVMe SSDs can generate a significant amount of heat, especially under heavy load, some models come with a heatsink or heat spreader to help dissipate heat. If you plan to use your NVMe SSD for sustained, write-intensive workloads, choosing a model with a good cooling solution is recommended.

Drive Type	Interface	Typical Read Speed	Typical Write Speed	Pros	Cons
HDD	SATA III	80-160 MB/s	80-160 MB/s	High capacity, low cost per GB	Slow, susceptible to physical damage, noisy
SATA SSD	SATA III	Up to 550 MB/s	Up to 520 MB/s	Fast, durable, silent, energy-efficient	More expensive than HDDs, lower maximum capacity
NVMe SSD	PCIe 3.0 x4	Up to 3500 MB/s	Up to 3000 MB/s	Extremely fast, excellent random access performance	More expensive than SATA SSDs, requires M.2 NVMe slot
NVMe SSD	PCIe 4.0 x4	Up to 7000 MB/s	Up to 5000 MB/s	Blazing fast, cutting-edge performance	More expensive than PCIe 3.0 SSDs, requires compatible CPU and motherboard
NVMe SSD	PCIe 5.0 x4	Up to 14,000 MB/s	Up to 12,000 MB/s	Fastest consumer storage available	Most expensive, requires compatible CPU and motherboard, generates significant heat

Choosing the Right Storage Solution for Your Build

Now that you understand the different types of storage drives available and their key specifications, let's discuss how to choose the right storage solution for your specific needs:

8. **Determine Your Budget:** Storage prices can vary widely depending on the type, capacity, and performance of the drive. Set a budget before you start shopping and allocate your funds accordingly.

9. **Assess Your Storage Needs:** Consider how much storage space you'll need for your operating system, applications, and data. If you plan to store a large library of games, photos, or videos, you'll need a higher-capacity drive.

10. **Prioritize Speed:** If you want the fastest possible boot times, application loading times, and overall system responsiveness, an SSD is a must-have. For the best performance, choose an NVMe SSD. If you're on a tighter budget, a SATA SSD is still a significant upgrade over an HDD.

11. **Consider a Multi-Drive Setup:** Many users opt for a multi-drive setup, using an SSD for the operating system and frequently used applications and an HDD for mass storage of less frequently accessed data like photos, videos, and music. This allows you to enjoy the speed benefits of an SSD without breaking the bank on a high-capacity model.

12. **Check Compatibility:** Make sure the storage drive you choose is compatible with your motherboard. If you're choosing an NVMe SSD, make sure your motherboard has an M.2 slot that supports the NVMe interface and the desired PCIe generation.

13. **Read Reviews:** Once you've narrowed down your choices, read reviews of specific models to see how they perform in real-world scenarios. Pay attention to factors

like sustained write performance, thermal management, and endurance.

Installing Your Storage Drives

The process of installing your storage drives will vary depending on the type of drive and your case. Here's a general overview:

Installing a 3.5-inch HDD:

10. Locate a 3.5-inch drive bay in your case. These are typically found in a drive cage near the front of the case.

11. Slide the HDD into the drive bay, aligning the screw holes on the drive with those on the cage.

12. Secure the drive to the cage using the appropriate screws (usually included with the case).

13. Connect one end of a SATA data cable to the SATA port on the HDD and the other end to a SATA port on the motherboard.

14. Connect a SATA power connector from the power supply to the power port on the HDD.

Installing a 2.5-inch SATA SSD:

1. Locate a 2.5-inch drive bay in your case. Some cases have dedicated 2.5-inch bays, while others require you to use an adapter to mount a 2.5-inch drive in a 3.5-inch bay.

2. Slide the SSD into the drive bay or adapter, aligning the screw holes.

3. Secure the drive using the appropriate screws.

4. Connect one end of a SATA data cable to the SATA port on the SSD and the other end to a SATA port on the motherboard.

5. Connect a SATA power connector from the power supply to the power port on the SSD.

Installing an M.2 NVMe SSD:

1. Locate the M.2 slot on your motherboard. It's usually found near the CPU or PCIe slots and may be covered by a heatsink or shield.

2. If necessary, remove the heatsink or shield covering the M.2 slot.

3. Align the notch on the M.2 SSD with the key in the M.2 slot.

4. Insert the SSD into the slot at a slight angle (usually around 30 degrees).

5. Gently press down on the other end of the SSD until it's parallel with the motherboard.

6. Secure the SSD using the small screw that came with your motherboard. Be careful not to overtighten the screw.

7. If your SSD or motherboard came with a heatsink, install it over the SSD according to the manufacturer's instructions.

8. Connect one end of a SATA data cable to the SATA port on the SSD and the other end to a SATA port on the motherboard.

Configuring Your Storage in the BIOS/UEFI and OS

After installing your storage drives, you'll need to configure them in your computer's BIOS/UEFI and operating system:

1. **Enter the BIOS/UEFI:** Restart your computer and press the appropriate key during the boot process to enter the BIOS/UEFI setup. This key is usually displayed on the screen during startup and is often Del, F2, F10, or F12.

2. **Set the Boot Order:** In the BIOS/UEFI, navigate to the boot settings and make sure your SSD (if you're using one for your OS) is set as the first boot device. This will ensure that your computer boots from the SSD instead of the HDD (if present).

3. **Enable NVMe (if applicable):** If you've installed an NVMe SSD, make sure that NVMe is enabled in the BIOS/UEFI settings. The exact location of this setting will vary depending on your motherboard, but it's often found in the advanced storage or PCIe settings.

4. **Save and Exit:** Save your changes and exit the BIOS/UEFI. Your computer will restart.

5. **Install the Operating System:** If you're installing a new operating system, boot from the installation media (e.g., a USB flash drive or DVD) and follow the on-screen instructions. When prompted to choose where to install the OS, select your SSD.

6. **Initialize and Format (if necessary):** If you've added a new, blank storage drive (either SSD or HDD) and it doesn't show up in your operating system, you may need to initialize and format it. In Windows, you can do this using the Disk Management utility. Right-click on the Start menu, select "Disk Management," and follow the prompts to initialize the disk, create a new partition, and format it with a file system (usually NTFS for Windows).

With your storage drives installed and configured, you're ready to enjoy the benefits of fast, reliable storage for your operating system, applications, and data. Whether you've chosen an HDD for mass storage, an SSD for speed, or an NVMe SSD for cutting-edge performance, you now have the foundation for a responsive and capable PC. In the next chapter, we'll move on to the power supply, the unsung hero that provides the necessary juice to keep all your components running smoothly.

CHAPTER SEVEN: Power Supplies (PSU): Fueling Your System Safely

You've now selected the core components that will make up your PC: the CPU, motherboard, RAM, graphics card, and storage drives. But there's one more crucial piece of the puzzle that often gets overlooked, yet is absolutely essential for a stable and reliable system: the Power Supply Unit, or PSU. The PSU is the unsung hero of your build, responsible for converting the AC power from your wall outlet into the various DC voltages that your components need to operate. Without a good quality PSU, your expensive components could be at risk of damage, and your system's stability could be compromised.

In this chapter, we'll dive deep into the world of power supplies. We'll explore the different types of PSUs, their key specifications, and the factors to consider when choosing the right one for your build. We'll also touch upon some common misconceptions and best practices for PSU selection and installation. By the end of this chapter, you'll have a thorough understanding of power supplies and be ready to choose a reliable and efficient unit to power your dream machine.

The Role of the PSU: Converting and Distributing Power

The power supply's primary function is to convert the alternating current (AC) power from your wall outlet into the direct current (DC) power that your computer's components require. It does this through a series of transformers, rectifiers, and filters that step down the voltage, convert it to DC, and smooth out any fluctuations.

A typical PC PSU provides several different DC voltage rails:

- **+12V:** The most important rail, providing power to the CPU, graphics card, and most other components. Modern systems rely heavily on the +12V rail, and a PSU's capacity on this rail is a key indicator of its overall quality and capability.

- **+5V:** Used by some older components and peripherals, but less important in modern systems.

- **+3.3V:** Used by some motherboard components and peripherals.

- **-12V:** A legacy rail that's rarely used in modern systems but is still included for compatibility with older components.

- **+5VSB (Standby):** Provides a small amount of power to the motherboard even when the computer is turned off, allowing for features like wake-on-LAN and USB charging when the system is in standby mode.

The PSU distributes these voltages to the various components through a set of cables and connectors. The main connectors include:

- **24-pin ATX:** The main power connector for the motherboard, providing +3.3V, +5V, +12V, -12V, and +5VSB.

- **4+4-pin EPS/ATX12V:** Provides additional +12V power to the CPU. Most modern CPUs require an 8-pin connector, but some high-end models may need more.

- **6+2-pin PCIe:** Provides +12V power to the graphics card. Most modern GPUs require one or more 6-pin or 8-pin PCIe connectors.

- **SATA:** Provides power to SATA storage drives (HDDs and SSDs) and other SATA devices.

- **Molex:** An older type of connector used for some peripherals and case fans.

- **Floppy:** A legacy connector that's rarely used in modern systems.

Wattage: How Much Power Do You Need?

One of the first things to consider when choosing a PSU is its wattage, which represents the maximum amount of power the unit can deliver to your components. It's crucial to choose a PSU that can provide enough power for all your components, with some headroom for future upgrades and to ensure stable operation under heavy load.

To determine your system's power requirements, you can use an online power supply calculator, such as the ones provided by OuterVision or Newegg. These calculators take into account the power consumption of your CPU, graphics card, motherboard, RAM, storage drives, and other components, and provide an estimated wattage for your system.

As a general rule, it's a good idea to choose a PSU with a wattage that's at least 20-30% higher than your estimated system power consumption. This provides a safety margin and allows for potential future upgrades. For example, if your estimated system power consumption is 400W, a 500-600W PSU would be a good choice.

Here's a rough guideline for PSU wattage based on system type:

- **Basic Office/Web Browsing PC:** 300-400W

- **Mid-Range Gaming PC:** 500-650W

- **High-End Gaming/Content Creation PC:** 750-850W

- **Enthusiast/Workstation PC:** 1000W or more

Keep in mind that these are just rough estimates, and your specific power requirements may vary depending on your components and usage.

Efficiency Ratings: 80 Plus and Beyond

Power supplies are not 100% efficient, meaning that some of the power they draw from the wall is lost as heat during the AC-to-DC conversion process. The efficiency of a PSU is typically expressed as a percentage, representing the ratio of DC power output to AC power input. For example, a PSU that delivers 400W of DC power while drawing 500W of AC power from the wall would have an efficiency of 80%.

The 80 Plus certification program was introduced in 2004 to promote energy efficiency in power supplies. To receive 80 Plus certification, a PSU must be at least 80% efficient at 20%, 50%, and 100% load, and have a power factor of 0.9 or higher at 100% load.

Over the years, the 80 Plus program has expanded to include several tiers of efficiency:

80 Plus Tier	Efficiency at 20% Load	Efficiency at 50% Load	Efficiency at 100% Load	Power Factor at 100% Load
80 Plus	80%	80%	80%	0.9
80 Plus Bronze	82%	85%	82%	0.9
80 Plus Silver	85%	88%	85%	0.9
80 Plus Gold	87%	90%	87%	0.9
80 Plus Platinum	90%	92%	89%	0.95
80 Plus Titanium	92%	94%	90%	0.95

Higher efficiency ratings generally mean that the PSU wastes less energy as heat, resulting in lower electricity bills and a cooler, quieter system. However, higher-rated PSUs also tend to be more expensive.

For most users, an 80 Plus Gold rated PSU offers a good balance of efficiency and cost. However, if you're building a high-end system or live in an area with high electricity costs, you might want to consider an 80 Plus Platinum or Titanium rated unit.

Form Factors: ATX, SFX, and More

Power supplies come in different form factors, which refer to their physical size and shape. The most common form factor for desktop PCs is ATX, which measures 150mm x 86mm x 140mm (width x height x depth). Most standard PC cases are designed to accommodate ATX power supplies.

However, there are also smaller form factors available for compact builds:

- **SFX:** Measuring 125mm x 63.5mm x 100mm, SFX PSUs are significantly smaller than ATX units and are designed for use in small form factor cases.

- **SFX-L:** A slightly longer version of SFX, measuring 125mm x 63.5mm x 130mm, allowing for a larger fan and potentially better cooling and quieter operation.

- **TFX:** A slim form factor measuring 85mm x 64mm x 175mm, often used in very compact or low-profile systems.

When choosing a PSU, make sure it's compatible with your case. Most standard cases support ATX power supplies, but smaller cases may require an SFX or SFX-L unit. Some cases come with adapters that allow you to use a smaller PSU in a larger form factor bay.

Modularity: Full, Semi, or Non-Modular

Power supply cables can be either fully modular, semi-modular, or non-modular:

- **Fully Modular:** All cables are detachable, allowing you to use only the cables you need and reducing cable clutter in your case. This can improve airflow and make for a cleaner-looking build.

- **Semi-Modular:** Some cables (usually the essential ones like the 24-pin ATX and 4+4-pin EPS/ATX12V) are permanently attached, while others are detachable.

- **Non-Modular:** All cables are permanently attached to the PSU. This can result in more cable clutter, especially if you don't need to use all the provided cables.

Fully modular PSUs are generally the most desirable, as they offer the greatest flexibility and the cleanest look. However, they also tend to be more expensive. Semi-modular PSUs offer a good compromise between flexibility and cost, while non-modular units are usually the most affordable but can be more challenging to work with in terms of cable management.

Single Rail vs. Multi-Rail: A Contentious Debate

One of the more contentious topics in the world of power supplies is the debate between single-rail and multi-rail designs. This refers to how the +12V power is distributed within the PSU.

14.   **Single Rail:** A single, high-capacity +12V rail provides power to all components. This design is simpler and can potentially deliver more power to a single component if needed.

15.   **Multi-Rail:** Multiple +12V rails, each with its own over-current protection (OCP) circuit, distribute power to different components. This design can potentially offer better protection against catastrophic failures, as a fault on one rail may not affect the others.

The debate centers around which design is safer and more reliable. Proponents of single-rail designs argue that they are less likely to experience issues with imbalanced loads and can provide more consistent power delivery. Proponents of multi-rail designs argue that they offer better protection against overloads and short circuits.

In practice, the difference between single-rail and multi-rail designs is often negligible for most users. Modern high-quality PSUs, whether single-rail or multi-rail, are designed to provide stable and reliable power to your components. The quality of the components and the overall design of the PSU are more important factors than the rail configuration.

Other Features to Consider

In addition to the key specifications discussed above, there are several other features you might want to consider when choosing a PSU:

15. **Fan Size and Type:** The size and type of fan used in the PSU can impact its cooling performance and noise levels. Larger fans (135mm or 140mm) can generally move more air at lower speeds than smaller fans (120mm), resulting in quieter operation. Some PSUs use fluid dynamic bearing (FDB) or magnetic levitation (maglev) fans, which are typically quieter and more durable than traditional sleeve bearing fans.

16. **Fan Control:** Some PSUs feature fanless or semi-fanless modes, where the fan only turns on when the PSU reaches a certain temperature or load threshold. This can result in near-silent operation under light loads.

17. **Cables and Connectors:** Make sure the PSU has the necessary cables and connectors for your components, including the appropriate number of 6+2-pin PCIe connectors for your graphics card(s) and SATA connectors for your storage drives. Some PSUs come with flat, ribbon-style cables, which can be easier to route and manage than traditional round cables.

18. **Protection Features:** A good quality PSU should have various protection features to safeguard your components against power issues, such as:

    a. **Over Voltage Protection (OVP):** Shuts down the PSU if the output voltage exceeds a certain threshold.

    b. **Under Voltage Protection (UVP):** Shuts down the PSU if the output voltage drops below a certain threshold.

    c. **Over Current Protection (OCP):** Shuts down the PSU if the current on a particular rail exceeds a certain limit.

    d. **Short Circuit Protection (SCP):** Shuts down the PSU if a short circuit is detected.

    e. **Over Power Protection (OPP):** Shuts down the PSU if the total power draw exceeds the PSU's rated capacity.

    f. **Over Temperature Protection (OTP):** Shuts down the PSU if the internal temperature gets too high.

19. **Warranty:** A longer warranty period generally indicates that the manufacturer has confidence in the PSU's quality and reliability. Most reputable PSU brands offer warranties of 5, 7, or even 10 years.

Choosing the Right PSU for Your Build

Now that you understand the key features and specifications of power supplies, let's discuss how to choose the right one for your specific needs:

6. **Calculate Your Power Needs:** Use an online power supply calculator to estimate your system's power consumption, taking into account all your components.

Add a 20-30% safety margin to determine the minimum wattage for your PSU.

7. **Choose an Efficiency Rating:** Select an appropriate 80 Plus efficiency rating based on your budget and priorities. For most users, an 80 Plus Gold rated PSU offers a good balance of efficiency and cost.

8. **Determine the Form Factor:** Make sure the PSU form factor (ATX, SFX, etc.) is compatible with your case.

9. **Decide on Modularity:** Choose between fully modular, semi-modular, or non-modular cables based on your preferences for cable management and budget.

10. **Consider Other Features:** Look for additional features that are important to you, such as fan size and type, fan control, cables and connectors, and protection features.

11. **Read Reviews:** Once you've narrowed down your choices, read reviews from reputable sources (e.g., Tom's Hardware, JonnyGURU, PC Perspective) to see how specific models perform in terms of efficiency, voltage regulation, ripple, noise, and overall quality.

12. **Check the Warranty:** Opt for a PSU with a longer warranty period from a reputable brand.

Installing Your Power Supply

Installing a power supply is a relatively straightforward process, but it's important to do it correctly to ensure proper operation and avoid damaging your components. Here's a step-by-step guide:

9. **Prepare Your Case:** Open your computer case and remove any existing power supply if you're replacing an old unit.

10.   **Mount the PSU:** Place the new power supply in the PSU bay of your case, aligning the screw holes. Secure the PSU to the case using the screws provided by the case or PSU manufacturer.

11.   **Connect the Cables:** If you're using a modular or semi-modular PSU, connect the necessary cables to the PSU before installing it in the case. This can make it easier to route the cables later.

12.   **Route the Cables:** Plan your cable routing to ensure a clean and organized build. Use cable ties or Velcro straps to secure the cables to the case and keep them out of the way of fans and other components.

13.   **Connect to the Motherboard:** Connect the 24-pin ATX cable to the main power connector on the motherboard. Connect the 4+4-pin EPS/ATX12V cable to the CPU power connector on the motherboard.

14.   **Connect to the Graphics Card:** If your graphics card requires additional power, connect the 6+2-pin PCIe cables to the appropriate connectors on the card.

15.   **Connect to Storage Drives:** Connect the SATA power cables to your SATA HDDs and SSDs. If you have any older devices that use Molex connectors, connect the appropriate cables.

16.   **Connect to Other Components:** Connect any other necessary cables, such as those for case fans or other peripherals.

17.   **Double-Check Connections:** Before powering on your system, double-check all your connections to make sure everything is properly seated and secure.

18. **Power On and Test:** Connect the power cord to the PSU and plug it into a wall outlet. Power on your system and make sure everything is working correctly.

With your power supply installed and your system up and running, you can rest assured that your components are receiving clean, stable power. A good quality PSU is an investment in the longevity and reliability of your PC, and by choosing the right one for your needs and installing it correctly, you've taken a crucial step towards building a solid and dependable system. In the next chapter, we'll move on to the case, the enclosure that houses all your carefully selected components and plays a vital role in cooling, aesthetics, and overall system organization.

CHAPTER EIGHT: Cases: Aesthetics, Airflow, and Size Considerations

You've now chosen all the core internal components that will make up your PC: the CPU, motherboard, RAM, graphics card, storage drives, and power supply. But you need a place to put all these carefully selected parts, and that's where the case comes in. The case is the enclosure that houses all your components, providing protection, organization, and cooling. But it's more than just a box; the case also plays a significant role in your system's aesthetics, airflow, and overall size.

In this chapter, we'll explore the world of PC cases. We'll look at the different types of cases available, the key features to consider, and how to choose the right one for your specific needs and preferences. We'll also discuss some best practices for case selection and offer tips on how to optimize your case for airflow and aesthetics. By the end of this chapter, you'll have a solid understanding of PC cases and be ready to choose the perfect home for your dream build.

The Role of the Case: More Than Just a Box

At its most basic level, the case is a container that holds all your PC components together. It provides a physical structure for mounting your motherboard, drives, and other hardware, and it protects these delicate components from dust, physical damage, and electromagnetic interference.

But the case does more than just house your components. It also plays a crucial role in:

1. **Airflow and Cooling:** The case is a critical part of your system's cooling solution. It provides pathways for air to flow through the system, carrying heat away from your components. The design of the case, including the number

and placement of fans, vents, and filters, can significantly impact your system's thermal performance.

2. **Aesthetics:** The case is the most visible part of your PC, and its design can make a big statement about your personal style and preferences. Cases come in a wide variety of shapes, sizes, colors, and materials, with features like tempered glass panels, RGB lighting, and unique designs that can make your build stand out.

3. **Organization:** A well-designed case provides features that help you organize your components and cables, making for a cleaner, more efficient build. This can include drive bays, cable routing channels, and tie-down points that help keep everything neat and tidy.

4. **Noise Reduction:** Some cases are specifically designed to minimize noise, with features like sound-dampening materials, solid panels, and low-noise fans. If you're building a PC for a quiet environment, such as a bedroom or home theater, a silent case can be a worthwhile investment.

5. **Expandability:** The case determines the size and number of components you can install in your system. Factors like the number of drive bays, expansion slots, and fan mounts can limit or enable future upgrades.

Case Sizes and Form Factors: Finding the Right Fit

One of the first things to consider when choosing a case is its size, which is typically determined by the form factor of the motherboard it's designed to accommodate. As we discussed in Chapter 3, the most common motherboard form factors are ATX, Micro-ATX, and Mini-ITX.

Cases are generally categorized by the largest motherboard size they can support. Here are the main types:

- **Full Tower:** These are the largest cases, typically designed to accommodate Extended ATX (E-ATX) and ATX motherboards, although some can also fit smaller form factors. Full tower cases offer the most space for components, with plenty of room for multiple graphics cards, large radiators, and numerous storage drives. They are a good choice for enthusiasts and power users who need maximum expandability and cooling potential. Full tower cases typically stand 22 inches or more in height.

- **Mid Tower:** These are the most common type of case and are designed to accommodate ATX motherboards, although most can also fit Micro-ATX and Mini-ITX boards. Mid tower cases offer a good balance of size, expandability, and cooling performance for most users. They typically have enough room for one or two graphics cards, several storage drives, and multiple fans or radiators. Mid tower cases usually stand between 18 and 22 inches tall.

- **Micro-ATX Tower:** These cases are designed specifically for Micro-ATX motherboards, although some can also fit Mini-ITX boards. They are smaller than mid tower cases but still offer decent expandability and cooling options. Micro-ATX towers are a good choice for users who want a more compact build without sacrificing too much on features or performance.

- **Mini-ITX Tower:** These are the smallest cases, designed for Mini-ITX motherboards. They are ideal for compact, space-saving builds, such as home theater PCs or small form factor gaming rigs. Mini-ITX cases typically have limited space for components and may require careful planning to ensure compatibility and adequate cooling.

In addition to these main types, there are also some less common form factors, such as:

- **Slim:** These cases are designed to be as thin as possible, often using low-profile expansion cards and smaller power supplies. They are typically used for basic office PCs or home theater PCs where space is at a premium.

- **Cube:** As the name suggests, these cases have a cube-like shape and often feature unique internal layouts. They can be a good choice for compact, stylish builds.

- **Open-Air/Test Bench:** These are not really cases in the traditional sense but rather open frames designed for easy access to components. They are often used by hardware reviewers or enthusiasts who frequently swap out parts.

When choosing a case size, it's important to consider your specific needs and preferences. If you want maximum expandability and cooling potential and don't mind a large footprint, a full tower case might be a good choice. If you want a more compact build but still need decent expandability, a mid tower or Micro-ATX tower could be a better fit. And if you're building a small form factor PC for a specific purpose, such as a home theater PC or a portable gaming rig, a Mini-ITX case might be the way to go.

It's also crucial to ensure that your chosen case is compatible with your components. Check the case's specifications for:

- **Motherboard Compatibility:** Make sure the case supports your motherboard's form factor (ATX, Micro-ATX, Mini-ITX, etc.).

- **Graphics Card Clearance:** Check the maximum graphics card length the case can accommodate, especially if you're using a long, high-end GPU.

- **CPU Cooler Clearance:** If you're using a large air cooler, make sure the case has enough clearance for its height.

- **Power Supply Compatibility:** Ensure the case supports your power supply's form factor (ATX, SFX, etc.) and has enough space for its length.

- **Drive Bays:** Check the number and type of drive bays (3.5-inch, 2.5-inch, 5.25-inch) to make sure the case can accommodate your storage needs.

Materials and Build Quality: From Budget to Premium

PC cases are made from a variety of materials, each with its own pros and cons in terms of durability, aesthetics, and cost. The most common materials are:

- **Steel:** Steel is the most common material used for PC cases, especially in budget and mid-range models. It's strong, durable, and relatively inexpensive. However, steel cases can be heavy, and cheaper steel cases may use thin panels that can feel flimsy and vibrate.

- **Aluminum:** Aluminum is lighter and more aesthetically pleasing than steel, with a premium look and feel. It's also a good conductor of heat, which can help with cooling. However, aluminum cases are typically more expensive than steel cases, and they can be more prone to scratches and dents.

- **Tempered Glass:** Tempered glass is increasingly popular for case panels, especially side panels. It offers a clear view of the internal components, allowing you to show off your build and any RGB lighting. Tempered glass is also scratch-resistant and easy to clean. However, it's heavier than plastic, more fragile, and can contribute to higher internal temperatures if not properly ventilated.

- **Plastic:** Plastic is often used for front panels, accents, and internal components in PC cases. It's lightweight, inexpensive, and can be molded into complex shapes.

However, cheaper plastic can look and feel cheap, and it's not as durable as metal.

The build quality of a case can vary widely depending on the materials used, the thickness of the panels, and the overall design and construction. Budget cases may use thin steel and plastic, with fewer features and less refined construction. Mid-range cases often use a mix of steel, plastic, and sometimes tempered glass, with better build quality and more features. Premium cases may use thicker steel, aluminum, and tempered glass, with excellent build quality, advanced features, and unique designs.

When choosing a case, it's worth considering the materials and build quality, especially if you plan to keep the case for multiple builds or if you want a premium look and feel. However, keep in mind that higher-quality materials and construction often come with a higher price tag.

Airflow and Cooling: Keeping Your Components Cool

One of the most important functions of a PC case is to provide adequate airflow to keep your components cool. The case's design, including the number and placement of fans, vents, and filters, can significantly impact your system's thermal performance.

Here are some key factors to consider when evaluating a case's airflow and cooling capabilities:

16. **Fan Mounts:** Most cases come with one or more pre-installed fans, and many have additional fan mounts that allow you to add more fans to improve airflow. Common fan sizes are 120mm and 140mm, with some cases supporting larger 200mm fans. When choosing a case, consider the number, size, and placement of the fan mounts, and make sure they are compatible with your cooling needs.

17. **Fan Configuration:** The way you configure your fans can have a big impact on airflow. The most common configuration is to have intake fans at the front or bottom

of the case, drawing in cool air, and exhaust fans at the rear or top, expelling hot air. This creates positive pressure inside the case, which can help to reduce dust buildup. However, some users prefer a negative pressure setup, with more exhaust fans than intake fans, which can be more effective at removing heat but may draw in more dust.

18.   **Vents and Grills:** The size, shape, and placement of vents and grills can affect airflow. Larger, less restrictive vents generally allow for better airflow, while smaller, more restrictive vents may impede airflow but can help to reduce noise and dust. Some cases have mesh panels or large perforated areas to maximize airflow.

19.   **Filters:** Dust filters are important for keeping the inside of your case clean and preventing dust buildup on your components, which can reduce their performance and lifespan. Look for cases with easily removable and washable filters, especially on intake fan mounts.

20.   **Radiator Support:** If you're planning to use a liquid cooler, make sure the case has enough space and mounting options for your radiator(s). Common radiator sizes are 120mm, 140mm, 240mm, 280mm, and 360mm. Some cases can accommodate even larger radiators or multiple radiators for extreme cooling setups.

21.   **Cable Management:** Good cable management can improve airflow by reducing obstructions and allowing air to flow more freely through the case. Look for cases with features like cable routing holes, tie-down points, and channels behind the motherboard tray to help keep your cables organized.

When choosing a case, it's important to consider your cooling needs based on your components and usage. If you're building a high-end system with a powerful CPU and graphics card, you'll likely need a case with excellent airflow and multiple fan mounts. If you're using a liquid cooler, make sure the case has adequate radiator support. And if you're building a silent PC, look for cases with sound-dampening materials and low-noise fans.

Aesthetics and Design: Making a Statement

For many PC builders, the case is more than just a functional enclosure; it's also a way to express their personal style and make a statement. Cases come in a wide variety of designs, colors, and styles, from sleek and minimalist to bold and aggressive.

Here are some aesthetic and design factors to consider when choosing a case:

20. **Color:** Cases are available in a wide range of colors, with black and white being the most common. Some cases come in other colors, such as red, blue, or green, or have colored accents. Choose a color that matches your personal preferences and the overall theme of your build.

21. **Windowed Panels:** Many cases feature a windowed side panel, typically made of tempered glass or acrylic, that allows you to see the internal components of your PC. This can be a great way to show off your hardware and any RGB lighting. Some cases have full tempered glass panels, while others have smaller windows or partial windows.

22. **RGB Lighting:** RGB lighting has become a popular feature in PC cases, allowing you to customize the look of your build with a wide range of colors and effects. Some cases come with built-in RGB lighting, while others have RGB fans or LED strips that can be controlled via software or a physical controller. If you're into RGB, look for cases with good lighting options and compatibility with your preferred RGB ecosystem (e.g., ASUS Aura Sync, MSI Mystic Light, Gigabyte RGB Fusion).

23. **Front Panel Design:** The front panel is one of the most visible parts of the case and can make a big impact on its overall look. Some cases have a minimalist front panel with a clean, simple design, while others have a more

aggressive or industrial look with angular shapes, mesh panels, or other design elements.

24.   **Unique Designs:** Some case manufacturers offer unique or unconventional designs that can make your build stand out. This can include cases with unusual shapes, unconventional layouts, or special features like built-in handles or modular components.

When choosing a case based on aesthetics, it's important to consider your personal preferences and the overall theme of your build. Do you want a sleek, minimalist look or a bold, eye-catching design? Do you prefer a specific color or material? Do you want to show off your components with a windowed panel or RGB lighting?

However, it's also important not to sacrifice functionality for aesthetics. Make sure the case you choose still meets your needs in terms of size, compatibility, airflow, and other practical considerations.

Other Features to Consider

In addition to the factors discussed above, there are several other features you might want to consider when choosing a PC case:

13.   **Front Panel I/O:** Most cases have a front panel I/O area with various ports and buttons, such as USB ports, audio jacks, power and reset buttons, and sometimes fan or RGB controllers. Consider the number and type of ports you need, and look for cases with convenient placement and easy access.

14.   **Drive Bays and Mounting Options:** Make sure the case has enough drive bays and mounting options for your storage needs. This includes 2.5-inch bays for SSDs, 3.5-inch bays for HDDs, and sometimes 5.25-inch bays for optical drives or other accessories. Some cases have tool-less drive installation mechanisms, which can make it easier to add or remove drives.

15.   **Cable Management Features:** Good cable management is important for both aesthetics and airflow. Look for cases with features like cable routing holes with rubber grommets, tie-down points, and channels behind the motherboard tray to help keep your cables organized. Some cases also have PSU shrouds or covers that can help to hide excess cables and create a cleaner look.

16.   **Tool-less Design:** Some cases feature tool-less designs that allow you to install or remove components without the need for tools. This can include tool-less drive bays, expansion slots, and side panels. Tool-less designs can make building and upgrading your PC quicker and easier.

17.   **Noise Reduction Features:** If you're building a silent PC, look for cases with noise reduction features like sound-dampening materials, solid panels, and low-noise fans. Some cases also have features like fan speed controllers or rubber grommets on fan mounts to help reduce vibration and noise.

18.   **Water Cooling Support:** If you're planning to use a custom water cooling loop, make sure the case has adequate space and mounting options for your radiators, pump, and reservoir. Some cases are specifically designed for water cooling and have features like dedicated pump mounts, fill and drain ports, and extra space for tubing.

19.   **Vertical GPU Mount:** Some cases offer a vertical GPU mount option, which allows you to mount your graphics card vertically instead of horizontally. This can be a great way to show off your GPU and can sometimes improve cooling performance. However, it may require a separate PCIe riser cable and can limit the use of other expansion slots.

Choosing the Right Case for Your Build

Now that you understand the key features and considerations for choosing a PC case, let's discuss how to select the right one for your specific needs:

19. **Determine Your Size and Form Factor:** Start by determining the appropriate size and form factor for your case based on your motherboard and other components. Consider your space constraints, expandability needs, and aesthetic preferences.

20. **Set a Budget:** PC cases can range in price from under $50 to over $500. Set a budget before you start shopping and consider how much you're willing to spend on a case. Keep in mind that while the case is an important part of your build, it's generally not where you want to allocate the majority of your budget.

21. **Prioritize Airflow and Cooling:** Make sure the case you choose has adequate airflow and cooling capabilities for your components. Consider the number and placement of fan mounts, the size and type of vents and filters, and the radiator support if you're using a liquid cooler.

22. **Consider Compatibility:** Ensure that the case is compatible with all your components, including your motherboard, graphics card, CPU cooler, power supply, and storage drives. Check the case's specifications for clearances and mounting options.

23. **Think About Aesthetics:** Choose a case that matches your personal style and the overall theme of your build. Consider factors like color, windowed panels, RGB lighting, and front panel design.

24. **Look for Useful Features:** Consider additional features that might be important to you, such as front panel I/O, drive bays and mounting options, cable management features, tool-less design, noise reduction, and water cooling support.

25. **Read Reviews:** Once you've narrowed down your choices, read reviews from reputable sources to see how specific cases perform in terms of build quality, airflow, noise, and ease of use. Look for reviews that test the case with similar components to your own.

26. **Consider Manufacturer Reputation:** Stick with reputable case manufacturers that have a good track record for quality and customer support. Some popular and well-regarded case brands include Fractal Design, NZXT, Corsair, Cooler Master, Phanteks, Lian Li, and be quiet!.

Case Type	Typical Motherboard Support	Pros	Cons
Full Tower	E-ATX, ATX, Micro-ATX, Mini-ITX	Maximum expandability and cooling potential, plenty of space for large components and multiple GPUs	Large footprint, can be expensive, may be overkill for most users
Mid Tower	ATX, Micro-ATX, Mini-ITX	Good balance of size, expandability, and cooling, suitable for most builds	May not have enough space for extreme builds with multiple GPUs or large radiators
Micro-ATX Tower	Micro-ATX, Mini-ITX	More compact than mid tower, still offers decent expandability and cooling	Less space for components than mid tower, may require more careful planning
Mini-ITX Tower	Mini-ITX	Smallest form factor, ideal for compact and portable builds	Limited space for components, may require specialized hardware, cooling can be a challenge

Building in Your Case: Tips and Best Practices

Once you've chosen your case and have all your components ready, it's time to start building. Here are some tips and best practices for building in your case:

7. **Prepare Your Workspace:** Make sure you have a clean, well-lit workspace with enough room to work comfortably. Gather all the necessary tools, such as screwdrivers, zip ties, and an anti-static wrist strap.

8. **Install the I/O Shield:** Before installing the motherboard, install the I/O shield that came with your motherboard into the back of the case. Make sure it's properly aligned and snapped into place.

9. **Install the Motherboard:** Carefully place the motherboard into the case, aligning it with the standoffs. Secure the motherboard to the case using the screws provided.

10. **Install the CPU, Cooler, and RAM:** If you haven't already, install the CPU, CPU cooler, and RAM onto the motherboard before installing it in the case. This can be easier to do when the motherboard is outside the case.

11. **Install the Power Supply:** Install the power supply into its designated bay in the case and secure it with screws. If you're using a modular or semi-modular PSU, connect the necessary cables to the PSU before installing it.

12. **Route the Cables:** Plan your cable routing and start connecting the power cables to the motherboard, graphics card, and other components. Use the case's cable management features, such as routing holes, tie-down points, and channels, to keep the cables organized and out of the way.

13. **Install the Graphics Card:** Install the graphics card into the appropriate PCIe slot on the motherboard and

secure it to the case. Connect the necessary power cables to the GPU.

14. **Install Storage Drives:** Install your storage drives into their respective bays or mounting locations in the case. Connect the power and data cables to the drives.

15. **Connect Front Panel I/O:** Connect the front panel I/O cables, such as USB, audio, and power/reset buttons, to the appropriate headers on the motherboard. Refer to your motherboard's manual for the correct pinouts.

16. **Install Fans and Radiators:** Install any additional fans or radiators according to your cooling plan. Connect the fans to the appropriate headers on the motherboard or to a fan controller.

17. **Double-Check Connections:** Before powering on your system, double-check all your connections to make sure everything is properly seated and secure. Make sure there are no loose cables or obstructions that could interfere with fans or other components.

18. **Power On and Test:** Connect the power cord to the PSU and plug it into a wall outlet. Power on your system and make sure everything is working correctly. Check the temperatures and fan speeds to ensure that your cooling is adequate.

The case is a crucial part of your PC build, providing a home for your components and playing a significant role in your system's cooling, aesthetics, and organization. By understanding the different types of cases available, the key features to consider, and how to choose the right one for your specific needs and preferences, you can select the perfect case to house your dream machine. With your case chosen and your components installed, you're well on your way to completing your PC build.

CHAPTER NINE: Cooling Solutions: Keeping Your PC Temperatures in Check

You've now selected all the core components of your PC: the CPU, motherboard, RAM, graphics card, storage drives, power supply, and case. But as you assemble your dream machine, there's one more critical aspect to consider: cooling. Modern PC components, especially high-performance CPUs and GPUs, generate significant amounts of heat. Without adequate cooling, this heat can lead to reduced performance, instability, and even permanent damage to your components.

In this chapter, we'll explore the world of PC cooling solutions. We'll look at the different types of cooling methods available, from air coolers to liquid coolers, and the key factors to consider when choosing the right cooling solution for your specific needs and budget. We'll also discuss some best practices for optimizing your cooling setup and monitoring your system's temperatures. By the end of this chapter, you'll have a solid understanding of PC cooling and be ready to choose the perfect solution to keep your system running cool and stable.

The Importance of Cooling: Why Heat is the Enemy

Before we dive into the specifics of cooling solutions, it's important to understand why heat management is so crucial for your PC's performance and longevity.

Heat is a natural byproduct of the electrical processes that occur within your computer's components. As electricity flows through the transistors and circuits of your CPU, GPU, and other parts, some of that energy is inevitably converted into heat. The more powerful the component and the harder it's working, the more heat it generates.

If this heat is not effectively dissipated, it can cause several problems:

1. **Thermal Throttling:** When a component gets too hot, it may automatically reduce its clock speed to lower heat output and prevent damage. This is known as thermal throttling. While it's an important safety mechanism, it also means reduced performance. Your CPU or GPU won't be able to run at its full potential if it's constantly overheating and throttling.

2. **Instability:** Excessive heat can cause system instability, leading to crashes, freezes, or other unpredictable behavior. This is because the electrical properties of components can change at high temperatures, causing errors or malfunctions.

3. **Reduced Lifespan:** Prolonged exposure to high temperatures can shorten the lifespan of your components. Heat can accelerate the degradation of the materials and structures within your CPU, GPU, and other parts, leading to premature failure.

4. **Noise:** To combat heat, your system's fans may need to spin at higher speeds, resulting in increased noise. If your cooling solution is inadequate, you may end up with a PC that's not only underperforming but also loud and distracting.

Understanding Heat Transfer: Conduction, Convection, and Radiation

To effectively cool your PC, it's helpful to understand the basic principles of heat transfer. There are three main mechanisms by which heat moves from one place to another:

- **Conduction:** This is the transfer of heat through direct contact between objects or substances. For example, when you touch a hot stove, heat is conducted from the stove to your hand. In a PC, conduction is used to transfer heat from the CPU or GPU to the cooler's heatsink.

- **Convection:** This is the transfer of heat through the movement of fluids (liquids or gases). In a PC, convection is primarily used to transfer heat from the heatsink to the surrounding air, which is then carried away by fans.

- **Radiation:** This is the transfer of heat through electromagnetic waves, such as infrared radiation. All objects emit some amount of heat through radiation, but it's generally a less significant factor in PC cooling compared to conduction and convection.

Most PC cooling solutions utilize a combination of conduction and convection to dissipate heat. The heat is conducted from the component to a heatsink, and then convection, aided by fans, carries the heat away from the heatsink and out of the system.

Air Cooling: The Traditional Approach

Air cooling is the most common and generally the most affordable method of cooling a PC. It uses a combination of heatsinks and fans to dissipate heat from the components into the surrounding air.

Heatsinks: Maximizing Surface Area

A heatsink is a passive component, typically made of aluminum or copper, that's designed to absorb and dissipate heat from a heat source, such as a CPU or GPU. The key to a heatsink's effectiveness is its large surface area. Heatsinks typically have a series of fins or pins that increase the surface area in contact with the air, allowing for more efficient heat transfer.

The base of the heatsink makes direct contact with the component being cooled, often with a layer of thermal paste in between to improve thermal conductivity. The heat is conducted from the component to the base of the heatsink and then spreads throughout the fins.

Fans: Creating Airflow

While a heatsink alone can dissipate some heat, it's much more effective when combined with a fan. The fan creates airflow over the heatsink's fins, carrying away the heat through convection.

PC fans typically come in sizes ranging from 80mm to 200mm, with 120mm and 140mm being the most common. Larger fans can generally move more air at lower speeds, resulting in quieter operation. However, the size of the fan is just one factor affecting its performance. Other important factors include the fan's blade design, motor type, and speed (measured in revolutions per minute, or RPM).

CPU Air Coolers: Keeping the Brain Cool

The CPU is one of the primary heat generators in a PC, and it typically requires a dedicated cooler. CPU air coolers come in a variety of shapes and sizes, from low-profile coolers designed for compact systems to large tower coolers with multiple fans for high-performance CPUs.

A typical CPU air cooler consists of a heatsink with a copper base and aluminum fins, one or more heat pipes that help to transfer heat from the base to the fins, and one or more fans that blow air through the fins.

When choosing a CPU air cooler, there are several factors to consider:

- **TDP Rating:** As we discussed in Chapter 2, Thermal Design Power (TDP) is a measure of the maximum amount of heat a CPU is expected to generate under typical usage. When choosing a cooler, make sure its TDP rating is equal to or higher than your CPU's TDP. This ensures that the cooler can adequately dissipate the heat generated by your CPU.

- **Socket Compatibility:** Make sure the cooler is compatible with your CPU's socket (e.g., LGA 1700 for Intel 12th/13th Gen, AM5 for AMD Ryzen 7000 series).

- **Size and Clearance:** Consider the size of the cooler and make sure it will fit in your case and won't interfere with other components, such as RAM or the graphics card. Large tower coolers can be quite tall and may not fit in smaller cases or may obstruct tall RAM modules.

- **Noise Level:** If you're building a quiet PC, look for a cooler with a low noise rating (measured in decibels, or dBA). Larger fans and fans with fluid dynamic bearings (FDB) or magnetic levitation (maglev) bearings tend to be quieter.

- **Aesthetics:** While not as important as performance, the look of the cooler can be a factor for some users. Some coolers come with RGB lighting or other aesthetic features.

Case Fans: Maintaining System-Wide Airflow

In addition to the CPU cooler, most PCs also use one or more case fans to maintain airflow throughout the system. Case fans help to draw in cool air from outside the case and exhaust hot air from inside the case, creating a constant flow of air that helps to cool all the components.

When choosing case fans, consider the following:

- **Size:** As mentioned earlier, common fan sizes are 120mm and 140mm. Larger fans can generally move more air at lower speeds, resulting in quieter operation. Make sure the fans you choose are compatible with the fan mounts in your case.

- **Airflow and Static Pressure:** Airflow, measured in cubic feet per minute (CFM), represents the amount of air a fan can move. Static pressure, measured in millimeters of water (mmH2O), represents the fan's ability to push air against resistance, such as a heatsink or radiator. For general case airflow, fans with higher CFM ratings are typically better. For cooling heatsinks or radiators, fans with higher static pressure ratings are more effective.

- **Noise Level:** As with CPU coolers, the noise level of case fans can be an important factor, especially if you're building a quiet PC. Look for fans with low dBA ratings and consider features like fluid dynamic bearings or anti-vibration mounts.

- **PWM Control:** Pulse Width Modulation (PWM) allows you to control the speed of a fan based on the temperature of a component, such as the CPU. This can help to keep your system quiet under light loads while still providing adequate cooling under heavy loads. Look for fans with 4-pin PWM connectors and make sure your motherboard has enough PWM fan headers.

Advantages and Disadvantages of Air Cooling

Air cooling has several advantages:

- **Affordability:** Air coolers are generally less expensive than liquid coolers, especially for entry-level and mid-range options.

- **Simplicity:** Air coolers are relatively simple to install and maintain, with no need for pumps, radiators, or coolant.

- **Reliability:** With fewer moving parts and no risk of leaks, air coolers can be more reliable in the long run.

- **Low Maintenance:** Air coolers typically require minimal maintenance, aside from occasional cleaning to remove dust buildup.

However, air cooling also has some disadvantages:

22. **Limited Cooling Capacity:** While high-end air coolers can perform on par with some liquid coolers, they may not be able to match the cooling capacity of high-end

liquid cooling solutions, especially for overclocked CPUs or in systems with multiple high-end GPUs.

23. **Size and Clearance Issues:** Large air coolers can be bulky and may not fit in smaller cases or may interfere with other components.

24. **Noise:** While many air coolers are designed to be quiet, they can still be louder than some liquid cooling solutions, especially under heavy load.

Liquid Cooling: Taking it to the Next Level

Liquid cooling, also known as water cooling, uses a liquid coolant to transfer heat away from components more efficiently than air cooling. While it's generally more expensive and complex than air cooling, liquid cooling can offer superior cooling performance and quieter operation, making it a popular choice for high-end builds and overclocking enthusiasts.

All-in-One (AIO) Liquid Coolers: The Easy Entry Point

All-in-One (AIO) liquid coolers, also known as closed-loop coolers, are the most common type of liquid cooling solution for PCs. They come pre-assembled and sealed from the factory, with a pump, radiator, tubing, and fans all included in one package.

Here's how an AIO liquid cooler works:

25. **Water Block:** A water block, which is essentially a heatsink with channels for liquid coolant, is mounted on the CPU. The base of the water block is typically made of copper for optimal thermal conductivity.

26. **Pump:** A small pump circulates the liquid coolant through the system. In most AIOs, the pump is integrated into the water block assembly.

27. **Tubing:** Flexible tubing carries the coolant from the water block to the radiator and back again.

28.   **Radiator:** The radiator is a large, finned heat exchanger that dissipates the heat from the coolant into the surrounding air. It's typically mounted on one of the case's fan mounts.

29.   **Fans:** One or more fans are mounted on the radiator to create airflow through the fins, similar to an air cooler's heatsink.

The coolant absorbs heat from the CPU as it passes through the water block. The pump then circulates the heated coolant to the radiator, where the heat is transferred to the fins and dissipated into the air by the fans. The cooled liquid then returns to the water block to repeat the cycle.

When choosing an AIO liquid cooler, consider the following:

20.   **Radiator Size:** AIO radiators typically come in sizes ranging from 120mm to 360mm, with some larger models available. The larger the radiator, the more surface area it has for heat dissipation, and the better the cooling performance. Make sure the radiator size you choose is compatible with your case's fan mounts.

21.   **Fan Configuration:** Most AIOs come with one or more fans for the radiator. As with case fans, consider the size, airflow, static pressure, and noise level of the included fans. Some AIOs allow you to replace the stock fans with your own for better performance or aesthetics.

22.   **Pump Performance:** While most AIO pumps are relatively quiet and reliable, some higher-end models offer more powerful pumps with adjustable speeds or other advanced features.

23.   **Tubing Length and Flexibility:** Make sure the tubing is long enough to reach from the CPU to your chosen radiator mounting location and flexible enough to allow for easy installation and routing.

24.   **Compatibility:** As with air coolers, make sure the AIO is compatible with your CPU socket and that your case has enough clearance for the radiator and fans.

Custom Liquid Cooling Loops: The Ultimate Cooling Solution

For the ultimate in cooling performance and customization, enthusiasts may opt for a custom liquid cooling loop. This involves assembling your own liquid cooling system from individual components, including a water block, pump, reservoir, radiator, tubing, fittings, and coolant.

Custom loops offer several advantages over AIOs:

27.   **Superior Cooling Performance:** With a custom loop, you can choose high-end components optimized for maximum cooling performance, such as thicker radiators, more powerful pumps, and specialized water blocks for CPUs, GPUs, and even other components like RAM or VRMs.

28.   **Greater Customization:** Custom loops allow for much greater customization in terms of aesthetics and layout. You can choose from a wide variety of components in different colors, materials, and styles to create a unique look that matches your build's theme.

29.   **Expandability:** Unlike AIOs, which are closed systems, custom loops can be expanded to cool multiple components or upgraded with new parts over time.

30.   **Quieter Operation:** With careful component selection and tuning, custom loops can often run quieter than AIOs, especially under heavy load.

However, custom loops also have some significant drawbacks:

19.   **Cost:** Custom loops are generally much more expensive than AIOs, with the cost of individual components quickly adding up.

20.   **Complexity:** Building a custom loop requires careful planning, research, and assembly. It's not recommended for beginners or those who are not comfortable working with potentially leak-prone components.

21.   **Maintenance:** Custom loops require periodic maintenance, such as flushing the coolant and cleaning the components, to ensure optimal performance and prevent issues like algae growth or corrosion.

22.   **Risk of Leaks:** While modern liquid cooling components are generally reliable, there's always a risk of leaks with a custom loop, which can potentially damage your PC's components if not caught and addressed quickly.

Building a custom loop is a complex topic that could fill a whole chapter on its own. If you're interested in pursuing this route, be prepared to do extensive research and consider seeking advice from experienced builders or online communities.

Other Cooling Methods: Exotic Solutions

While air and liquid cooling are the most common methods for cooling PCs, there are some other, more exotic solutions that are occasionally used by enthusiasts or for specialized applications:

1. **Passive Cooling:** Passive cooling relies on heatsinks alone, with no fans, to dissipate heat. This can result in a completely silent system, but it's generally only suitable for low-power components or specialized applications where noise is a primary concern.

2. **Sub-Ambient Cooling:** This involves using a cooling method that can bring the temperature of the components below the ambient room temperature. Examples include:

   o **Phase-Change Cooling:** Similar to a refrigerator, phase-change coolers use a compressor to circulate a refrigerant that absorbs heat from the CPU or

GPU and dissipates it through a condenser. These systems can achieve very low temperatures but are expensive, bulky, and consume a lot of power.

- o **Thermoelectric Cooling (TEC) / Peltier:** TEC coolers use the Peltier effect to create a temperature difference between two sides of a ceramic plate. One side gets cold and is used to cool the component, while the other side gets hot and is cooled by a heatsink or liquid cooler. TECs can achieve sub-ambient temperatures but are not very efficient and can generate significant amounts of heat on the hot side.

- o **Liquid Nitrogen (LN2) / Dry Ice:** For extreme overclocking, enthusiasts may use cryogenic cooling methods like liquid nitrogen or dry ice to cool the CPU or GPU to extremely low temperatures. This is typically done for short benchmarking runs rather than for everyday use.

These exotic cooling methods are generally not practical or necessary for most users. They can be expensive, complex, power-hungry, and may even pose risks to your components if not used correctly.

Choosing the Right Cooling Solution for Your Build

Now that you understand the different types of cooling solutions available, let's discuss how to choose the right one for your specific needs:

1. **Consider Your CPU and TDP:** The first step is to consider your CPU and its TDP rating. This will determine the minimum cooling capacity you need. For low to mid-range CPUs, a good air cooler may be sufficient. For high-end CPUs or overclocking, an AIO liquid cooler or a high-end air cooler may be a better choice.

2. **Assess Your Budget:** Cooling solutions can range in price from under $30 for a basic air cooler to over $500 for a high-end custom loop. Set a budget before you start shopping and consider how much you're willing to spend on cooling.

3. **Think About Your Case:** Make sure the cooling solution you choose is compatible with your case in terms of size, clearance, and mounting options. Consider the airflow design of your case and the number and placement of fan mounts.

4. **Evaluate Your Noise Tolerance:** If you're building a quiet PC, pay attention to the noise levels of the coolers and fans you're considering. Look for low dBA ratings and features like fluid dynamic bearings or PWM control.

5. **Decide Between Air and Liquid Cooling:** Based on your budget, performance needs, and comfort level with installation and maintenance, decide whether to go with an air cooler or a liquid cooler. For most users, a good air cooler or an AIO liquid cooler will be sufficient.

6. **Consider Aesthetics:** While performance should be your primary concern, you may also want to consider the aesthetics of your cooling solution. Some coolers come with RGB lighting or other visual features that can enhance the look of your build.

7. **Read Reviews:** Once you've narrowed down your choices, read reviews from reputable sources to see how specific models perform in terms of cooling, noise, and ease of installation.

Optimizing Your Cooling Setup

Once you've chosen and installed your cooling solution, there are several steps you can take to optimize its performance:

1. **Properly Apply Thermal Paste:** When installing your CPU cooler, make sure to apply thermal paste correctly. Use a high-quality paste and apply a thin, even layer to the CPU's integrated heat spreader (IHS). Too much or too little paste can negatively impact heat transfer.

2. **Optimize Fan Placement and Airflow:** Experiment with different fan configurations to find the optimal airflow setup for your case. Generally, you want to have intake fans at the front or bottom of the case and exhaust fans at the rear or top. Use cable ties or other cable management features to keep cables out of the airflow path.

3. **Set Fan Curves:** Use your motherboard's BIOS or fan control software to set appropriate fan curves for your CPU cooler and case fans. You want the fans to spin fast enough to provide adequate cooling under load but not so fast that they're unnecessarily loud at idle.

4. **Clean Regularly:** Dust buildup can significantly impact cooling performance over time. Periodically clean your case's dust filters and use compressed air to remove dust from heatsinks, fans, and other components.

5. **Monitor Temperatures:** Use monitoring software, such as HWMonitor or Core Temp, to keep an eye on your CPU and GPU temperatures, especially under load. This can help you identify potential cooling issues and adjust your fan curves or other settings as needed.

6. **Consider Ambient Temperature:** Keep in mind that the ambient temperature of the room your PC is in can affect cooling performance. If possible, try to keep your PC in a cool, well-ventilated area.

Cooling Method	Pros	Cons	Typical Use Case
Air Cooling	<ul><li>Affordable</li><li>Simple to install</li><li>Reliable</li><li>Low maintenance</li></ul>	<ul><li>Limited cooling capacity</li><li>Size and clearance issues</li><li>Can be noisy under load</li></ul>	<ul><li>Entry-level to mid-range builds</li><li>Systems with moderate TDP CPUs</li><li>Users who prioritize simplicity and affordability</li></ul>
AIO Liquid Cooling	<ul><li>Better cooling performance than air cooling</li><li>More compact than large air coolers</li><li>Quieter than many air coolers</li><li>Relatively easy to install</li></ul>	<ul><li>More expensive than air cooling</li><li>Potential for pump noise or failure</li><li>Limited customization and expandability</li></ul>	<ul><li>Mid-range to high-end builds</li><li>Overclocked CPUs</li><li>Users who want better cooling performance without the complexity of a custom loop</li></ul>

Cooling Method	Pros	Cons	Typical Use Case
Custom Liquid Cooling	• Superior cooling performance • Highly customizable • Expandable to cool multiple components • Potentially very quiet operation	• Expensive • Complex to install and maintain • Risk of leaks • Requires periodic maintenance	• High-end and enthusiast builds • Extreme overclocking • Users who want maximum cooling performance and customization

Cooling is a critical aspect of any PC build, especially for high-performance systems. By understanding the different types of cooling solutions available, the key factors to consider when choosing a cooler, and how to optimize your cooling setup, you can ensure that your PC runs cool, stable, and at its full potential. With your cooling solution selected and installed, you're one step closer to completing your dream build.

CHAPTER TEN: Essential Tools and Workspace Preparation

You've now chosen all the components for your dream PC: the CPU, motherboard, RAM, graphics card, storage drives, power supply, case, and cooling solution. You're eager to start putting it all together, but before you dive into the assembly process, there's one more crucial step: preparing your workspace and gathering the necessary tools. Building a PC is a hands-on process that requires a suitable workspace and a few basic tools. Having everything organized and ready ahead of time will make the building process smoother, safer, and more enjoyable.

In this chapter, we'll discuss the essential tools you'll need for PC building, as well as some optional but helpful additions. We'll also cover how to prepare your workspace to ensure a clean, safe, and efficient building experience. By the end of this chapter, you'll be ready to set up your building area and gather the tools you need to assemble your PC with confidence.

Essential Tools: The Must-Haves

While PC building doesn't require an extensive or expensive toolkit, there are a few essential tools that you'll need to assemble your components properly:

1. **Screwdrivers:** A good set of screwdrivers is the most important tool for PC building. You'll need them to install various components, such as the motherboard, drives, and power supply. The most commonly used type is a Phillips-head screwdriver, specifically a #2 size. It's a good idea to have a set that includes a #1 and #0 size as well, as some smaller screws may require these. Magnetic tips are highly recommended, as they make it easier to handle small screws and prevent them from falling into hard-to-reach places inside the case.

○ Recommendation: A good starter set is the iFixit Mako Driver Kit - 64 Precision Bits.

2. **Anti-Static Wrist Strap:** This is a simple but crucial tool for preventing electrostatic discharge (ESD), which can potentially damage sensitive electronic components. The wrist strap grounds you to the case, dissipating any static electricity that may have built up on your body. While the risk of ESD damage is relatively low with modern components, it's still a good practice to use a wrist strap, especially if you're working in a dry or carpeted environment.

○ Recommendation: Theনিয়া Static Vastar ESD Anti-Static Wrist Strap is a good choice.

3. **Thermal Paste:** If you're installing a new CPU cooler, you'll likely need to apply thermal paste to the CPU's integrated heat spreader (IHS). Thermal paste helps to improve heat transfer between the CPU and the cooler by filling in any microscopic gaps between the two surfaces. Some coolers come with pre-applied thermal paste, but it's always a good idea to have some extra on hand.

○ Recommendation: Arctic MX-4 or Noctua NT-H1 are highly regarded thermal pastes.

4. **Zip Ties or Velcro Straps:** These are essential for cable management, which is important for both aesthetics and airflow. Zip ties are a simple and inexpensive way to bundle cables together and secure them to the case. Velcro straps offer a reusable and adjustable alternative.

○ Recommendation: The Cable Matters Assorted Cable Ties set offers a variety of sizes.

5. **Flashlight or Headlamp:** A good light source is crucial for seeing what you're doing inside the case, especially when working in tight spaces or with small components. A

flashlight or headlamp can help you illuminate your workspace and make it easier to align screws, connect cables, and identify components.

> o Recommendation: The GearLight LED Headlamp is a good hands-free option.

Optional but Helpful Tools: Making the Job Easier

In addition to the essential tools listed above, there are several other tools that can make the PC building process easier and more efficient:

- **Screwdriver Extension:** A flexible screwdriver extension can be helpful for reaching screws in tight or awkward places, such as those behind drive cages or under large CPU coolers.

  > o Recommendation: The Neiko Flexible Shaft Bit Extension is well made.

- **Magnetic Parts Tray:** A magnetic parts tray or bowl can help you keep track of small screws and other components during the building process. The magnets prevent the parts from rolling away or getting lost.

  > o Recommendation: The HORUSDY Magnetic Tray is good value for the money.

- **Tweezers or Pliers:** A pair of fine-tipped tweezers or needle-nose pliers can be useful for handling small components, such as jumpers or connectors, or for retrieving dropped screws from hard-to-reach places.

  > o Recommendation: The Hakko CHP-170 Micro Cutter is recommended by many PC builders.

- **Compressed Air:** A can of compressed air can be helpful for cleaning dust from components or the case before or during the building process. It's also useful for cleaning your PC periodically after it's built.

> o Recommendation: The Falcon Dust-Off is a good compressed air option.

- **Isopropyl Alcohol and Lint-Free Cloth:** Isopropyl alcohol (90% or higher) and a lint-free cloth can be used to clean thermal paste from the CPU or cooler, or to remove fingerprints or smudges from components.

> o Recommendation: MG Chemicals Isopropyl Alcohol and a microfiber cloth will do the job.

- **Multi-Bit Screwdriver:** A multi-bit screwdriver with interchangeable bits can be a convenient all-in-one solution for PC building. Look for one with a good selection of Phillips and flathead bits, as well as magnetic tips.

> o Recommendation: The Klein Tools 32500 is used by many technicians.

- **Scissors or Wire Cutters:** A pair of scissors or wire cutters can be useful for cutting zip ties or trimming excess cable length.

- **Small Container for Screws:** Using a small container, such as an egg carton, pill organizer, or ice cube tray, to store and organize the various screws that come with your case and components can be very helpful.

- **Gloves:** While not strictly necessary, wearing gloves can help prevent fingerprints and smudges on your components, especially if you have particularly oily skin. Some people also prefer to wear gloves to protect their hands from sharp edges inside the case. If you choose to wear gloves, make sure they are anti-static and fit snugly to allow for dexterity.

o Recommendation: The Maxiflex 34-874 is an anti-static glove that many technicians use.

Workspace Preparation: Creating a Safe and Efficient Building Environment

Before you start assembling your PC, it's important to prepare your workspace to ensure a safe, clean, and efficient building experience. Here are some tips for setting up your building area:

- **Choose a Suitable Location:** Select a well-lit, spacious, and static-free area to build your PC. A large table or desk is ideal. Avoid working on carpeted floors if possible, as they can generate static electricity. If you must work on carpet, consider using an anti-static mat in addition to your wrist strap.

- **Clear the Area:** Remove any clutter or unnecessary items from your workspace to give yourself plenty of room to work. Make sure you have enough space to lay out all your components, tools, and the case.

- **Ground Yourself:** Before handling any components, make sure to ground yourself using an anti-static wrist strap. Attach the clip to an unpainted metal part of the case to create a continuous ground path.

- **Organize Your Components:** Lay out all your components in an organized manner, grouping similar items together. This will make it easier to find what you need during the building process. You may want to keep the components in their anti-static bags until you're ready to install them.

- **Have the Manuals Handy:** Keep the manuals for your motherboard, case, and other components within easy reach. These manuals contain important information about installation procedures, connector locations, and other specifications.

- **Protect Delicate Surfaces:** If you're working on a surface that could be easily scratched or damaged, such as a finished wood table, consider placing a protective layer underneath, such as a large piece of cardboard, a rubber mat, or an old towel.

- **Ensure Good Lighting:** Make sure your workspace is well-lit, using overhead lighting and/or a desk lamp or headlamp. Good lighting is crucial for seeing small components and connectors, aligning screws, and working inside the case.

- **Keep Food and Drinks Away:** Avoid having food or drinks near your workspace while building your PC. Spilled liquids can damage electronic components, and crumbs or other food particles can create a mess and potentially cause problems if they get inside the case.

- **Take Breaks:** Building a PC can be a time-consuming process, especially if it's your first time. Remember to take breaks when needed to avoid fatigue and maintain focus. It's better to take your time and do things correctly than to rush and make mistakes.

Safety Considerations: Protecting Yourself and Your Components

While building a PC is generally a safe activity, there are a few safety considerations to keep in mind:

- **Electrostatic Discharge (ESD):** As mentioned earlier, ESD can potentially damage sensitive electronic components. Always use an anti-static wrist strap and ground yourself before handling any components. Avoid touching the metal contacts or circuitry on components unless necessary.

- **Sharp Edges:** Some cases may have sharp edges, especially around the drive bays or expansion slots. Be careful when reaching inside the case and consider wearing gloves to protect your hands.

- **Proper Lifting Techniques:** PC cases and some components, such as power supplies and large coolers, can be heavy. Use proper lifting techniques when moving these items to avoid strain or injury. Lift with your legs, not your back, and ask for help if something is too heavy to lift comfortably on your own.

- **Ventilation:** Some components, such as the CPU and GPU, can generate significant heat during operation. Make sure your workspace is well-ventilated to prevent heat buildup and ensure that your system has adequate airflow once it's assembled.

- **Avoid Over-tightening Screws:** When installing components, be careful not to over-tighten the screws. Over-tightening can strip the threads or damage the components. Use just enough force to secure the component firmly in place.

- **Read the Manuals:** Before installing any component, always read the corresponding section in the manual. The manuals contain important information about installation procedures, compatibility, and safety precautions.

- **Double-Check Connections:** Before powering on your system for the first time, double-check all your connections to make sure everything is properly seated and secured. This includes power cables, data cables, fan connectors, and front panel connectors.

- **Power Supply Safety:** The power supply is the only component in your PC that deals directly with high-voltage electricity. Never open the power supply casing, as this can expose you to dangerous voltages. If you suspect a problem with your power supply, replace it rather than attempting to repair it yourself.

Preparing for Software Installation

In addition to preparing your physical workspace and gathering the necessary tools, it's also a good idea to prepare for the software installation process before you start building your PC. This includes:

- **Creating Installation Media:** If you're installing a new operating system, such as Windows 10 or Windows 11, you'll need to create installation media, such as a bootable USB drive. You can download the necessary files and create the installation media using Microsoft's Media Creation Tool.

- **Downloading Drivers:** Before you start building, download the latest drivers for your motherboard, graphics card, and other components from the manufacturers' websites. Save these drivers to a USB drive so you can install them after you've installed the operating system. This is especially important for network drivers, as you won't be able to access the internet to download them after the build if you don't have network connectivity.

- **Backing Up Important Data:** If you're transferring data from an old PC to your new build, make sure to back up any important files before you start. You can use an external hard drive, cloud storage, or other backup methods to secure your data.

Conclusion

Preparing your workspace and gathering the necessary tools is an essential step in the PC building process. By having the right tools on hand and setting up a clean, safe, and organized building area, you can make the assembly process smoother, more efficient, and more enjoyable. Remember to use an anti-static wrist strap to prevent electrostatic discharge, take your time and read the manuals carefully, and double-check all your connections before powering on your system.

With your workspace prepared and your tools assembled, you're now ready to start building your dream PC. In the next chapter, we'll begin the assembly process, starting with installing the motherboard and CPU. Get ready to dive in and start putting those carefully selected components together!

CHAPTER ELEVEN: Installing the Motherboard and CPU

You've meticulously selected each component for your dream PC, from the powerful CPU and feature-rich motherboard to the high-speed RAM, cutting-edge graphics card, lightning-fast storage, reliable power supply, stylish case, and efficient cooling solution. You've also prepared your workspace and gathered all the necessary tools. Now, the moment has finally arrived to begin assembling your PC. In this chapter, we'll start with two of the most crucial steps: installing the motherboard and the CPU.

The motherboard serves as the foundation of your entire system, and the CPU is its brain. Properly installing these components is essential for ensuring a stable and well-functioning PC. While the process may seem daunting at first, it's actually quite straightforward if you follow the steps carefully and take your time. So, let's dive in and start bringing your dream machine to life.

Preparing the Motherboard: Out of the Box and Ready to Go

Before you begin, make sure your workspace is clean, well-lit, and static-free. Wear your anti-static wrist strap and connect it to an unpainted metal part of your case to ground yourself.

1. **Unboxing the Motherboard:** Carefully remove the motherboard from its anti-static bag and place it on a non-conductive surface. The box it came in can serve this purpose. Avoid placing it directly on the anti-static bag, as the exterior of the bag can sometimes conduct static electricity.

2. **Inspecting the Motherboard:** Take a moment to visually inspect the motherboard for any signs of damage, such as bent pins in the CPU socket, loose components, or scratches on the PCB. If you notice any damage, contact

the retailer or manufacturer immediately. It's much easier to address these issues before you start installing components.

3. **Installing the I/O Shield:** Locate the I/O shield that came with your motherboard. This is a rectangular metal plate with cutouts for the various ports on the back of the motherboard. Align the I/O shield with the corresponding opening on the back of your case and press it firmly into place until it snaps in. Make sure it's securely installed and properly aligned, as it can be difficult to adjust once the motherboard is in place. Some higher-end motherboards come with a pre-installed I/O shield, in which case you can skip this step.

Installing the CPU: Seating the Brain of Your PC

With the motherboard prepared, it's time to install the CPU. This is a delicate process, as the CPU socket contains many small, fragile pins that can be easily bent or damaged. Handle the CPU with care and follow these steps closely:

- **Identifying the CPU Socket:** Locate the CPU socket on your motherboard. It's usually a large, square socket with a lever on one side. The socket type will vary depending on your CPU and motherboard (e.g., LGA 1700 for Intel 12th/13th Gen, AM5 for AMD Ryzen 7000 series).

- **Opening the Socket:** Gently lift the lever on the side of the socket until it's in the fully open position. This will release the socket's retention mechanism. For Intel CPUs, there will also be a plastic or metal cover over the socket that needs to be lifted. AMD CPUs typically don't have this cover.

- **Aligning the CPU:** Carefully remove the CPU from its packaging, holding it by the edges. Avoid touching the pins or contacts on the bottom of the CPU. Locate the alignment indicators on the CPU and the socket. These are usually small triangles or notches that help you orient the CPU correctly.

- o **Intel CPUs:** Intel CPUs have two notches on the sides that align with corresponding tabs in the socket. The CPU will also have a small triangle in one corner that aligns with a triangle on the socket.

- o **AMD CPUs:** AMD CPUs have a small triangle in one corner that aligns with a triangle on the socket.

- **Inserting the CPU:** Gently lower the CPU into the socket, making sure the alignment indicators are properly matched. The CPU should drop into place without any force. Do not press down on the CPU. If it doesn't seem to be fitting correctly, double-check the alignment and try again.

- **Closing the Socket:** Once the CPU is seated in the socket, gently lower the lever back into its original position. You may feel some resistance as the lever engages the retention mechanism, especially with Intel sockets. This is normal, but if you feel excessive resistance, stop and double-check that the CPU is properly seated. For Intel CPUs, the plastic socket cover should pop off automatically as you lower the lever.

- **Inspecting the Installation:** Once the lever is fully closed, visually inspect the CPU to make sure it's sitting flat and even in the socket. There should be no gaps or unevenness.

Installing the CPU Cooler: Keeping Your Processor Cool

With the CPU installed, the next step is to install the CPU cooler. As we discussed in Chapter 9, the cooler is essential for dissipating the heat generated by the CPU and keeping it running at a safe temperature.

The installation process for CPU coolers can vary depending on the type and model of the cooler. In this section, we'll cover the general steps for installing an air cooler and an AIO liquid cooler. Always refer to the cooler's manual for specific instructions.

Installing an Air Cooler

- **Preparing the Cooler:** Remove the cooler from its packaging and familiarize yourself with its components. This typically includes the heatsink, one or more fans, mounting brackets, and thermal paste.

- **Applying Thermal Paste:** If your cooler doesn't have pre-applied thermal paste, you'll need to apply it to the CPU's integrated heat spreader (IHS). Squeeze a small, pea-sized amount of thermal paste onto the center of the IHS. Some users prefer to spread the paste into a thin, even layer using a plastic card or spreader, while others let the pressure of the cooler spread the paste. Either method can work, but the key is to use a small amount and ensure even coverage.

- **Mounting the Cooler:** The process for mounting the cooler will vary depending on the specific model and your CPU socket type. Generally, it involves the following steps:

  o **Attaching the Mounting Brackets:** Most air coolers use a set of mounting brackets that attach to the motherboard around the CPU socket. These brackets provide the necessary mounting points for the cooler. Refer to the cooler's manual to determine which brackets to use for your socket type and how to install them. This usually involves placing a backplate on the underside of the motherboard and screwing in standoffs or brackets from the top side.

  o **Positioning the Cooler:** Carefully place the cooler onto the CPU, aligning the mounting holes on the cooler with the standoffs or brackets on the motherboard.

o **Securing the Cooler:** Depending on the cooler's design, you'll either screw it directly into the standoffs or use a set of clips or levers to secure it to the mounting brackets. Apply even pressure as you tighten the screws or engage the clips, alternating between opposite corners to ensure even mounting pressure. Refer to the cooler's manual for the recommended tightening sequence and torque.

- **Connecting the Fan(s):** Once the cooler is securely mounted, connect the fan's power cable to the CPU_FAN header on the motherboard. If your cooler has multiple fans, you may need to use a splitter cable or connect the additional fans to other fan headers on the motherboard. Refer to your motherboard's manual for the location of the fan headers.

Installing an AIO Liquid Cooler

- **Preparing the Radiator and Fans:** Remove the AIO cooler from its packaging and attach the fans to the radiator using the provided screws. Pay attention to the orientation of the fans, as you'll want them to either push air through the radiator (if mounting it as an exhaust) or pull air through it (if mounting it as an intake).

- **Mounting the Radiator:** Choose a suitable location in your case to mount the radiator, such as the front, top, or rear fan mounts. Secure the radiator to the case using the provided screws. Make sure there's enough clearance for the tubing to reach the CPU socket without being stretched or kinked.

- **Applying Thermal Paste:** As with air coolers, apply a small, pea-sized amount of thermal paste to the center of the CPU's IHS if your AIO doesn't have pre-applied paste.

- **Mounting the Water Block:** The process for mounting the water block will vary depending on the specific AIO model and your CPU socket type. Generally, it involves the following steps:

- o **Attaching the Mounting Brackets:** Most AIOs use a set of mounting brackets that attach to the motherboard around the CPU socket. These brackets provide the necessary mounting points for the water block. Refer to the AIO's manual to determine which brackets to use for your socket type and how to install them.

- o **Positioning the Water Block:** Carefully place the water block onto the CPU, aligning the mounting holes on the block with the standoffs or brackets on the motherboard.

- o **Securing the Water Block:** Depending on the AIO's design, you'll either screw the water block directly into the standoffs or use a set of clips or levers to secure it to the mounting brackets. Apply even pressure as you tighten the screws or engage the clips, alternating between opposite corners to ensure even mounting pressure.

- **Connecting the Pump and Fans:** Connect the pump's power cable to the CPU_FAN or AIO_PUMP header on the motherboard. Connect the radiator fans to the CPU_OPT or other fan headers on the motherboard, or to a fan controller if your AIO includes one. Refer to your motherboard's manual for the location of the fan headers.

Installing the Motherboard into the Case: Bringing it All Together

With the CPU and cooler installed, it's time to install the motherboard into the case. This involves aligning the motherboard with the standoffs in the case and securing it with screws.

- **Preparing the Case:** Open your case and locate the motherboard standoffs. These are small, threaded posts that screw into the case and provide mounting points for the motherboard. Most cases come with standoffs pre-installed for the most common motherboard sizes, but you may need to add or remove standoffs depending on your motherboard's form factor. Refer to your case's manual to determine the correct standoff configuration for your motherboard.

- **Lowering the Motherboard into the Case:** Carefully lower the motherboard into the case, aligning the I/O panel with the I/O shield at the back of the case. Gently guide the motherboard onto the standoffs, making sure the mounting holes on the motherboard align with the standoffs in the case.

- **Securing the Motherboard:** Once the motherboard is in place, secure it to the standoffs using the screws provided with your case. Start with the center screw to hold the motherboard in place, then work your way outwards, tightening each screw a little at a time in a diagonal pattern to ensure even pressure. Don't overtighten the screws, as this can damage the motherboard.

- **Double-Checking Alignment:** Once all the screws are in place, double-check that the motherboard is properly aligned with the I/O shield and that there are no gaps between the motherboard and the standoffs. Also, make sure that no part of the motherboard is touching the case directly, as this could cause a short circuit.

Connecting the Front Panel Connectors: Power, Reset, and More

With the motherboard installed, it's time to connect the front panel connectors. These small cables connect the power button, reset button, power LED, hard drive activity LED, and front panel audio and USB ports to the motherboard.

25.   **Identifying the Connectors:** Locate the front panel connectors on your case. They are usually a set of small, individual connectors labeled with their function (e.g., PWR_SW, RESET_SW, PWR_LED, HDD_LED, HD Audio, USB).

26.   **Consulting the Motherboard Manual:** Refer to your motherboard's manual to identify the location and pinout of the front panel headers. These are usually located along the bottom edge of the motherboard and are labeled with their corresponding functions.

27.   **Connecting the Power and Reset Switches:** Connect the PWR_SW and RESET_SW connectors to their respective headers on the motherboard. The polarity of these connectors usually doesn't matter, but consult your motherboard's manual to be sure.

28.   **Connecting the LEDs:** Connect the PWR_LED and HDD_LED connectors to their respective headers on the motherboard. Pay attention to the polarity of these connectors, as LEDs only work in one direction. The positive and negative pins are usually indicated on the motherboard and the connectors. If you're not sure, consult your motherboard's manual.

29.   **Connecting the Audio and USB Ports:** Connect the HD Audio and USB connectors to their respective headers on the motherboard. These connectors are usually keyed, meaning they can only be inserted in one orientation. Make sure to align the connectors properly and gently push them into place. Refer to your motherboard's manual for the location and pinout of these headers.

Best Practices for Motherboard and CPU Installation

To ensure a smooth and successful installation of your motherboard and CPU, keep the following best practices in mind:

30. **Take Your Time:** Don't rush the installation process. Take your time to carefully read the manuals, align the components properly, and double-check your work. It's better to go slowly and get it right the first time than to rush and make mistakes that could damage your components.

31. **Handle Components with Care:** The CPU and motherboard are delicate components that can be easily damaged. Handle them with care, avoiding touching the pins or contacts, and always use an anti-static wrist strap to prevent electrostatic discharge.

32. **Use the Right Tools:** Make sure you have the right tools for the job, such as a Phillips-head screwdriver with a magnetic tip, an anti-static wrist strap, and thermal paste. Using the wrong tools can make the installation process more difficult and increase the risk of damaging components.

33. **Apply Even Pressure:** When installing the CPU cooler or securing the motherboard, apply even pressure to avoid damaging the components or creating uneven contact. Tighten screws in a diagonal pattern, a little at a time, to distribute the pressure evenly.

34. **Consult the Manuals:** Always refer to the manuals for your motherboard, CPU cooler, and case for specific instructions and diagrams. The manuals contain important information about installation procedures, compatibility, and safety precautions.

35. **Don't Force Anything:** If a component doesn't seem to be fitting correctly, don't force it. Stop and double-check the alignment and orientation. Forcing a component into place can damage the pins, sockets, or connectors.

36. **Keep Your Workspace Clean:** A clean and organized workspace can help prevent accidents and make

the building process more efficient. Keep your tools and components organized, and make sure you have enough space to work comfortably.

Installing the motherboard and CPU is a critical step in the PC building process. By carefully following the steps outlined in this chapter and taking your time, you can ensure that these essential components are properly installed and ready to power your dream machine. With the motherboard and CPU in place, you're well on your way to completing your build. In the next chapter, we'll move on to installing the RAM modules, another crucial step in assembling your PC.

CHAPTER TWELVE: Mounting the CPU Cooler

With your motherboard and CPU installed, along with your RAM modules in place, it's time to turn your attention to one of the most critical components for maintaining the health and performance of your processor: the CPU cooler. As we discussed in Chapter 9, the CPU generates a significant amount of heat during operation, and it's essential to dissipate that heat effectively to prevent thermal throttling, instability, and potential damage to the chip.

In this chapter, we'll focus on the practical steps of mounting your chosen CPU cooler. Whether you've opted for an air cooler or an all-in-one (AIO) liquid cooler, the process involves careful preparation, precise alignment, and secure attachment to ensure optimal thermal contact and efficient heat transfer. While the specific steps may vary slightly depending on the make and model of your cooler, we'll cover the general principles and best practices that apply to most installations.

Before you begin, make sure you have your cooler's manual readily available, as it contains detailed instructions and diagrams specific to your model. It's also a good idea to have your motherboard manual handy, as it provides information about the CPU socket area and any clearance considerations.

Preparing for Installation: Getting Everything Ready

Before you start mounting the cooler, take a few moments to prepare your workspace and components:

1. **Clean the CPU's Integrated Heat Spreader (IHS):** If you've previously installed a cooler or if there's any residue on the CPU's IHS, it's important to clean it thoroughly before applying new thermal paste. Use a lint-free cloth or a coffee filter and a small amount of isopropyl alcohol (90% or higher) to gently wipe the surface of the IHS until

it's clean and shiny. Allow any remaining alcohol to evaporate completely before proceeding.

2. **Gather Your Tools and Components:** Make sure you have all the necessary tools for installing your cooler, such as a screwdriver, thermal paste (if not pre-applied), and any mounting brackets or hardware that came with the cooler. Organize these items within easy reach so you don't have to search for them during the installation process.

3. **Read the Manual:** Familiarize yourself with the cooler's installation instructions by reading the manual thoroughly. Pay close attention to the diagrams and any specific steps or precautions mentioned for your CPU socket type.

4. **Test Fit (Optional):** If you're using a large air cooler, it can be helpful to do a test fit before applying thermal paste. This involves carefully placing the cooler on the CPU (without thermal paste) to check for any clearance issues with nearby components, such as RAM modules or VRM heatsinks. It also allows you to get a feel for the mounting process and identify any potential challenges.

Applying Thermal Paste: The Crucial Interface

Thermal paste, also known as thermal compound or thermal grease, is a thermally conductive substance that's applied between the CPU's IHS and the cooler's baseplate. Its purpose is to fill in any microscopic air gaps between the two surfaces, ensuring optimal heat transfer from the CPU to the cooler.

While some coolers come with pre-applied thermal paste, many users prefer to apply their own, either to use a higher-quality paste or to ensure proper coverage. If your cooler doesn't have pre-applied paste, or if you choose to use your own, here's how to apply it:

- **Choose a Method:** There are several methods for applying thermal paste, and the best one is often debated among PC enthusiasts. Here are three common approaches:

  - **Pea-Sized Dot:** Squeeze a small, pea-sized amount of thermal paste onto the center of the CPU's IHS. The pressure from mounting the cooler will spread the paste outwards.

  - **Line:** Apply a thin line of thermal paste across the center of the IHS. The orientation of the line can vary depending on the CPU and cooler design, but it's often recommended to align it with the longest dimension of the IHS.

  - **Spread:** Use a plastic card, a specialized spreader tool, or a gloved finger to manually spread the thermal paste into a thin, even layer across the entire surface of the IHS. This method can be more challenging to do correctly and risks introducing air bubbles if not done carefully.

  Regardless of the method you choose, the goal is to use a small amount of paste and achieve even coverage without excess.

- **Apply the Paste:** Carefully apply the thermal paste to the center of the IHS using your chosen method. If you're using the pea-sized dot or line method, be careful not to use too much paste. A small amount goes a long way, and excess paste can actually hinder heat transfer or even spill over onto the motherboard.

Mounting an Air Cooler: Step-by-Step

The process for mounting an air cooler can vary depending on the specific make and model, but the general steps are as follows:

- **Prepare the Mounting Brackets:** Most air coolers use a set of mounting brackets that attach to the motherboard around the CPU socket. These brackets provide the necessary mounting points for the cooler. Consult your cooler's manual to determine which brackets to use for your socket type and how to install them. This usually involves placing a backplate on the underside of the motherboard and screwing in standoffs or brackets from the top side. Some coolers may require you to remove the stock cooler mounting brackets that came with your motherboard.

- **Position the Cooler:** Carefully place the cooler onto the CPU, aligning the mounting holes on the cooler with the standoffs or brackets on the motherboard. Make sure the cooler is oriented correctly, with the fan(s) facing the desired direction for airflow.

- **Secure the Cooler:** Depending on the cooler's design, you'll either screw it directly into the standoffs or use a set of clips or levers to secure it to the mounting brackets. Apply even pressure as you tighten the screws or engage the clips, alternating between opposite corners to ensure even mounting pressure. This helps to create optimal contact between the cooler's baseplate and the CPU's IHS. Refer to your cooler's manual for the recommended tightening sequence and torque. It's important not to overtighten the screws, as this can damage the motherboard or the CPU.

- **Connect the Fan(s):** Once the cooler is securely mounted, connect the fan's power cable to the CPU_FAN header on the motherboard. If your cooler has multiple fans, you may need to use a splitter cable or connect the additional fans to other fan headers on the motherboard. Consult your motherboard's manual for the location of the fan headers and their corresponding labels.

Mounting an AIO Liquid Cooler: Step-by-Step

The process for mounting an AIO liquid cooler is slightly different from that of an air cooler, as you'll need to install both the radiator and the water block:

- **Prepare the Radiator and Fans:** Attach the fans to the radiator using the provided screws. Pay attention to the orientation of the fans, as you'll want them to either push air through the radiator (if mounting it as an exhaust) or pull air through it (if mounting it as an intake). Most users opt to mount the radiator as an exhaust, either at the top or rear of the case, to expel hot air directly out of the system.

- **Mount the Radiator:** Choose a suitable location in your case to mount the radiator, such as the front, top, or rear fan mounts. Secure the radiator to the case using the provided screws. Make sure there's enough clearance for the tubing to reach the CPU socket without being stretched or kinked. Also, ensure that the radiator and fans don't interfere with other components, such as the graphics card or RAM modules.

- **Prepare the Water Block:** Most AIOs use a mounting bracket system similar to air coolers. Consult your AIO's manual to determine which brackets to use for your socket type and how to install them on the water block.

- **Position the Water Block:** Carefully place the water block onto the CPU, aligning the mounting holes on the block with the standoffs or brackets on the motherboard. Make sure the water block is oriented correctly, with the tubing extending towards the radiator.

- **Secure the Water Block:** Depending on the AIO's design, you'll either screw the water block directly into the standoffs or use a set of clips or levers to secure it to the mounting brackets. Apply even pressure as you tighten the screws or engage the clips, alternating between opposite corners to ensure even mounting pressure. Refer to your

AIO's manual for the recommended tightening sequence and torque.

- **Connect the Pump and Fans:** Connect the pump's power cable to the CPU_FAN or AIO_PUMP header on the motherboard. If your motherboard doesn't have a dedicated AIO_PUMP header, you can use the CPU_FAN header or a regular SYS_FAN header. Connect the radiator fans to the CPU_OPT or other fan headers on the motherboard, or to a fan controller if your AIO includes one. Consult your motherboard's manual for the location of the fan headers and their corresponding labels.

Double-Checking Your Work: Ensuring a Secure Mount

After mounting your CPU cooler, take a moment to double-check your work:

- **Verify Even Pressure:** Gently press down on the cooler (for air coolers) or the water block (for AIOs) to ensure that it's making even contact with the CPU's IHS. There should be no wobbling or looseness.

- **Check for Clearance:** Make sure that the cooler and its fans don't interfere with other components, such as RAM modules, the graphics card, or VRM heatsinks. If you're using tall RAM modules, you may need to adjust the fan position on the cooler or use low-profile RAM.

- **Inspect the Tubing (for AIOs):** Ensure that the tubing is not kinked, twisted, or stretched. It should have a smooth, gentle curve from the water block to the radiator.

- **Confirm Fan Connections:** Double-check that all fan and pump power cables are securely connected to the appropriate headers on the motherboard.

Post-Installation Steps: Finishing the Job

With the cooler mounted and everything double-checked, there are a few final steps to complete:

30. **Tidy Up Cables:** Use zip ties or Velcro straps to manage the fan and pump power cables, keeping them neat and out of the way of other components. This not only improves aesthetics but also helps to maintain good airflow within the case.

31. **Reinstall Other Components:** If you removed any components, such as the graphics card or RAM modules, to make room for the cooler installation, reinstall them now.

32. **Power On and Test:** With everything in place, it's time to power on your system and test the cooler. Enter the BIOS/UEFI and monitor the CPU temperature to ensure that it's within the expected range for your CPU and cooler. You can also use monitoring software within your operating system to keep an eye on temperatures under load.

33. **Adjust Fan Curves (Optional):** Depending on your preferences and the noise levels of your cooler, you may want to adjust the fan curves in the BIOS/UEFI or using fan control software. This allows you to fine-tune the balance between cooling performance and noise levels.

Troubleshooting Common Issues

If you encounter any issues after installing your CPU cooler, here are a few common problems and their potential solutions:

37. **High CPU Temperatures:** If your CPU temperatures are higher than expected, consider the following:

   a. **Thermal Paste Application:** Make sure you applied thermal paste correctly, using a small amount and achieving even coverage.

b. **Mounting Pressure:** Verify that the cooler is securely mounted with even pressure. If it's loose or uneven, re-mount the cooler, paying careful attention to the tightening sequence and torque.

c. **Fan Orientation:** Double-check that the fans are oriented correctly to create proper airflow through the heatsink or radiator.

d. **Ambient Temperature:** Keep in mind that high ambient temperatures can impact cooling performance. Make sure your room is adequately ventilated.

38.   **Excessive Noise:** If your cooler is louder than expected, consider the following:

a. **Fan Curves:** Adjust the fan curves in the BIOS/UEFI or using fan control software to reduce fan speeds at lower temperatures.

b. **Fan Quality:** If you're using the stock fans that came with your cooler, they may not be the quietest option. Consider replacing them with higher-quality, low-noise fans.

c. **Vibration:** Make sure the cooler and its fans are securely mounted and that there are no loose screws or components that could be causing vibration.

39.   **System Instability:** If your system is experiencing crashes, freezes, or other stability issues, consider the following:

a. **Thermal Throttling:** Monitor your CPU temperatures under load to see if the CPU is thermal throttling. If it is, you may need to improve your cooling solution or reduce your overclock settings.

b. **Memory Compatibility:** If you're using tall RAM modules, make sure they're not interfering with the cooler. Try reseating the RAM or adjusting the fan position on the cooler.

c. **Power Supply:** In rare cases, an inadequate or failing power supply can cause system instability. Make sure your power supply is sufficient for your components and in good working order.

Mounting the CPU cooler is a critical step in the PC building process. By carefully preparing your components, applying thermal paste correctly, and securely mounting the cooler, you can ensure optimal thermal performance and keep your CPU running cool and stable. Remember to consult your cooler's manual for specific instructions and to double-check your work before powering on your system. With the CPU cooler in place, you're one step closer to completing your build. In the next chapter, we'll tackle another essential step: installing the RAM modules.

CHAPTER THIRTEEN: Installing RAM Modules

With the motherboard, CPU, and CPU cooler successfully installed, you've laid a solid foundation for your PC build. Now it's time to populate those memory slots and give your system the short-term memory it needs to run applications and process data efficiently. In this chapter, we'll focus on installing the RAM modules, a process that's relatively straightforward but requires careful attention to detail to ensure proper seating and optimal performance.

Random Access Memory, or RAM, is where your computer stores the data it's actively using. This includes the operating system, applications, and any files you have open. Unlike long-term storage like your SSD or HDD, RAM is volatile, meaning its contents are erased when the power is turned off. However, it's much faster than any long-term storage, allowing the CPU to quickly access the data it needs without being bottlenecked by slower storage speeds.

Before you begin, make sure you have your RAM modules readily available, along with your motherboard's manual. The manual contains important information about the specific RAM configuration and installation procedures for your motherboard model. It's also a good idea to have your anti-static wrist strap on and connected to an unpainted metal part of your case to prevent any electrostatic discharge from damaging the delicate RAM modules.

Understanding RAM Modules: A Quick Recap

As we discussed in Chapter 4, RAM modules come in different types, speeds, and capacities. Modern PCs typically use DDR4 or DDR5 RAM, with DDR4 being the more common and affordable option, while DDR5 offers higher performance at a premium price.

Each RAM module has a specific number of pins and a unique notch that prevents it from being inserted into an incompatible slot. DDR4 modules have 288 pins and a single notch, while DDR5 modules have 288 pins but with a notch that is positioned differently compared to DDR4. It's crucial to ensure that your RAM modules are compatible with your motherboard's supported memory type and speed.

RAM modules also come in different capacities, ranging from 4GB to 64GB or more per module. The total amount of RAM you need depends on your usage, with 16GB being a good starting point for most users, while 32GB or more is recommended for demanding applications and multitasking.

Identifying the RAM Slots: Locating the Memory Banks

RAM slots are located on the motherboard, usually to the right of the CPU socket. Most motherboards have two or four RAM slots, although some high-end models may have eight. The slots are typically color-coded to indicate the proper configuration for dual-channel or quad-channel operation, which we'll discuss later in this chapter.

The RAM slots have small latches or clips on either end that are used to secure the modules in place. These clips need to be in the open position before you can insert a RAM module. To open the clips, gently push them outwards away from the slot until they click into the open position.

Preparing the RAM Modules: Out of the Package and Ready for Action

Carefully remove your RAM modules from their packaging, handling them by the edges to avoid touching the gold contacts or the black memory chips. It's a good practice to keep the modules in their anti-static packaging until you're ready to install them to minimize the risk of electrostatic discharge.

Before inserting a module, inspect it for any visible damage, such as cracks, scratches, or bent pins. If you notice any damage, do not attempt to install the module, as it could damage your motherboard or cause system instability. Contact the retailer or manufacturer for a replacement.

Installing the RAM Modules: A Step-by-Step Guide

With the RAM slots identified and the modules prepared, you're ready to begin the installation process. Follow these steps carefully:

1. **Open the RAM Slot Clips:** Ensure that the clips on either end of the RAM slots are in the open position. Gently push them outwards until they click open.

2. **Align the RAM Module:** Hold the RAM module by its edges, with the notch on the bottom edge facing downwards. Align the notch on the module with the corresponding key in the RAM slot. This ensures that the module is inserted in the correct orientation. DDR4 and DDR5 modules have different notch positions, so they cannot be installed in the wrong type of slot.

3. **Insert the Module:** Gently but firmly insert the RAM module into the slot, applying even pressure to both ends of the module. The module should slide into the slot with relatively little resistance. As you press down, the clips on either end of the slot should automatically engage and snap into place, securing the module. You should hear a distinct click when the clips lock in.

4. **Verify Proper Seating:** Once the module is installed, visually inspect it to ensure that it's fully seated in the slot. The clips should be fully engaged, and the module should be level and even with no gaps between the module and the slot. Gently tug on the module to make sure it's securely in place.

5. **Repeat for Other Modules:** If you're installing multiple RAM modules, repeat steps 2-4 for each module. Pay close attention to the color-coding of the slots and your

motherboard's manual to ensure that you're installing the modules in the correct slots for optimal dual-channel or quad-channel performance.

Dual-Channel and Quad-Channel Configurations: Optimizing Memory Performance

Most modern motherboards support dual-channel or quad-channel memory configurations. These configurations allow the CPU to access multiple RAM modules simultaneously, effectively doubling or quadrupling the memory bandwidth compared to a single-channel configuration. This can result in significant performance improvements, especially in memory-intensive applications.

To take advantage of dual-channel or quad-channel operation, you need to install your RAM modules in the correct slots. The specific configuration varies depending on the motherboard, so it's crucial to consult your motherboard's manual for the recommended setup.

Here's a general overview of common configurations:

- **Dual-Channel with Two Modules:** On most motherboards with four RAM slots, you'll typically install two modules in slots A2 and B2 (the second and fourth slots from the CPU) to enable dual-channel operation. These slots are often color-coded to make them easy to identify.

- **Dual-Channel with Four Modules:** If you're installing four modules on a dual-channel motherboard, you'll typically populate all four slots.

- **Quad-Channel with Four Modules:** On motherboards that support quad-channel, you'll usually install four modules in slots A1, B1, C1, and D1 to enable quad-channel operation.

- **Quad-Channel with Eight Modules:** If you're using a high-end motherboard with eight RAM slots and want to run a quad-channel configuration, you'll typically populate all eight slots.

It's important to note that while it's technically possible to mix and match RAM modules of different capacities, speeds, and timings, it's generally not recommended. Doing so can lead to compatibility issues, instability, or reduced performance. For optimal results, it's best to use identical modules, preferably from a matched kit that's been tested and guaranteed to work together.

Troubleshooting RAM Installation: Addressing Common Issues

While RAM installation is usually straightforward, you may occasionally encounter issues. Here are some common problems and their potential solutions:

- **System Won't Boot or POST:** If your system fails to boot or complete the Power-On Self-Test (POST) after installing new RAM, try the following:

  - **Reseat the Modules:** Power off the system, unplug the power cable, and carefully reseat the RAM modules, ensuring they're fully inserted and the clips are engaged.

  - **Test with One Module:** Try booting with only one RAM module installed at a time, testing each module individually in each slot. This can help identify if one of the modules or slots is faulty.

  - **Clear CMOS:** Clearing the CMOS (Complementary Metal-Oxide-Semiconductor) can sometimes resolve compatibility issues. This involves either using a jumper on the motherboard or removing the CMOS battery for a few minutes.

Consult your motherboard's manual for the specific procedure.

  o **Check Compatibility:** Ensure that your RAM modules are compatible with your motherboard in terms of type (DDR4/DDR5), speed, and capacity. Refer to your motherboard's QVL (Qualified Vendor List) for a list of tested and approved RAM modules.

- **System Instability or Blue Screens:** If your system experiences crashes, freezes, or blue screens after installing new RAM, consider the following:

  o **Run MemTest86:** MemTest86 is a free, bootable memory testing utility that can help identify errors or instability in your RAM. Download the utility, create a bootable USB drive, and run the test for several hours or overnight to thoroughly check your RAM.

  o **Adjust RAM Settings in BIOS:** If you've manually adjusted your RAM settings in the BIOS, such as the speed or timings, try reverting to the default settings or using the XMP/DOCP profile (if available) to ensure stability.

  o **Check for Overheating:** While rare, overheating can sometimes cause RAM instability. Make sure your RAM modules have adequate airflow and are not obstructed by other components.

- **Incorrect RAM Capacity or Speed:** If your system is not recognizing the full capacity or speed of your RAM, try the following:

  o **Check BIOS Settings:** Enter the BIOS and verify that the RAM is detected correctly and running at the expected speed. If not, adjust the settings manually or enable the XMP/DOCP profile.

○ **Update BIOS:** In some cases, a BIOS update may be necessary to improve RAM compatibility or support higher capacities/speeds. Check your motherboard manufacturer's website for the latest BIOS version and follow the instructions for updating.

Post-Installation Steps: Verifying and Optimizing

Once you've successfully installed your RAM modules and your system is booting without issues, there are a few additional steps you can take to verify the installation and optimize performance:

- **Check System Information:** In your operating system, check the system information to verify that the full capacity of your RAM is recognized and that it's running in the correct configuration (e.g., dual-channel or quad-channel). In Windows, you can do this by right-clicking the Start button, selecting "System," and looking for the "Installed RAM" section.

- **Enable XMP/DOCP:** If your RAM modules support XMP (Extreme Memory Profile) or DOCP (Direct Over Clock Profile), you can enable this feature in the BIOS to automatically configure the RAM to run at its rated speed and timings. This can provide a performance boost without the need for manual tweaking.

- **Monitor Temperatures:** While RAM typically doesn't generate as much heat as the CPU or GPU, it's still a good idea to monitor its temperature, especially if you're overclocking or using high-performance modules. You can use monitoring software like HWMonitor or HWiNFO to check RAM temperatures.

- **Stress Test:** To ensure the stability of your RAM, especially if you've enabled XMP/DOCP or manually adjusted settings, it's a good idea to run a stress test. MemTest86, as mentioned earlier, is a popular choice for memory testing. Prime95 is another option that can stress test both the CPU and RAM.

Installing RAM modules is a crucial step in building your own PC. By carefully following the steps outlined in this chapter, you can ensure that your RAM is properly installed, configured for optimal performance, and running stably. With your motherboard, CPU, cooler, and RAM in place, you're well on your way to completing your build.

CHAPTER FOURTEEN: Installing the Graphics Card

With your motherboard, CPU, cooler, and RAM installed, you're making great progress on your PC build. Now it's time to tackle one of the most exciting components for gamers and creative professionals: the graphics card. The graphics card, also known as the GPU (Graphics Processing Unit), is responsible for rendering all the visuals you see on your screen, from the operating system's interface to the latest games and video editing applications.

In this chapter, we'll guide you through the process of installing your graphics card. While it might seem intimidating, especially with some of the larger, more powerful cards on the market, it's a relatively straightforward process. We'll cover everything you need to know, from preparing your case and identifying the correct slot to securing the card and connecting the necessary power cables.

Before you begin, make sure you have your graphics card, your case manual, and your motherboard manual readily available. It's also a good idea to wear your anti-static wrist strap to prevent any electrostatic discharge from damaging your components.

Understanding the Graphics Card: A Quick Recap

As we discussed in Chapter 5, the graphics card is a specialized processor designed to handle the complex calculations required for rendering images, videos, and 3D graphics. Modern graphics cards are essentially mini-computers themselves, with their own processor (the GPU), memory (VRAM), and cooling system.

Graphics cards come in various sizes, performance levels, and power requirements. High-end cards are typically larger, more powerful, and require more power connectors, while entry-level and mid-range cards are usually smaller and more power-efficient. It's crucial to ensure that your case has enough space to accommodate your chosen card and that your power supply has the necessary connectors and wattage to support it.

Identifying the PCI Express (PCIe) Slot: Finding the Right Home

Graphics cards connect to the motherboard via the PCI Express (PCIe) interface, which provides a high-speed connection for data transfer between the card and the rest of the system. Most modern motherboards have at least one PCIe x16 slot, which is the primary slot used for graphics cards.

The PCIe x16 slot is usually the longest expansion slot on the motherboard and is often located closest to the CPU. It may be a different color from the other slots to make it easier to identify. Some motherboards have multiple PCIe x16 slots, which can be used for installing multiple graphics cards in an SLI (NVIDIA) or CrossFire (AMD) configuration, although this is becoming less common with newer generations of GPUs.

It's important to note that while most graphics cards use a PCIe x16 interface, they don't necessarily utilize all 16 lanes. Some cards may use x8 or even x4 interfaces, especially in lower-end models. However, they will still physically fit into a x16 slot.

Preparing the Case: Making Room for the Card

Before you can install your graphics card, you need to prepare your case by removing the appropriate expansion slot covers. These are the small metal or plastic covers that block the openings at the back of the case where the graphics card's ports will be accessible.

1. **Identify the Correct Slot Covers:** Determine which expansion slots correspond to the PCIe x16 slot you'll be using. This is usually the top one or two slots, depending on the size of your graphics card. Most cards are dual-slot, meaning they take up the space of two expansion slots, but some high-end cards can be triple-slot or even larger.

2. **Remove the Slot Covers:** Depending on your case, the expansion slot covers may be secured with screws, clips, or a tool-less mechanism. Remove the screws or disengage the clips to remove the appropriate slot covers. Be careful not to damage the surrounding metal or plastic parts of the case.

3. **Set Aside the Screws or Clips:** If your slot covers were secured with screws or clips, set them aside in a safe place. You'll need them later to secure the graphics card.

Installing the Graphics Card: A Step-by-Step Guide

With the case prepared, you're ready to install your graphics card. Follow these steps carefully:

- **Align the Card:** Hold the graphics card by its edges, avoiding touching the gold contacts or any components on the card itself. Align the card's PCIe connector with the PCIe x16 slot on the motherboard. The ports on the card (e.g., HDMI, DisplayPort) should face the back of the case, where you removed the expansion slot covers.

- **Insert the Card:** Gently but firmly press the graphics card into the PCIe slot. Apply even pressure along the top edge of the card until it's fully seated. You should hear a click when the retention clip at the end of the slot engages, securing the card in place.

- **Secure the Card:** Once the card is fully inserted, use the screws or clips that you removed from the expansion slot covers to secure the card's bracket to the case. This helps to support the weight of the card and prevent it from sagging or coming loose over time. Tighten the screws or engage the clips firmly, but be careful not to overtighten.

- **Connect the Power Cables:** Most modern graphics cards require additional power beyond what the PCIe slot can provide. This is supplied through 6-pin, 8-pin, or 12-pin

PCIe power connectors. Consult your graphics card's manual to determine the specific power requirements.

- o Locate the appropriate power connectors on your power supply. They are usually labeled "PCIe" or "VGA."

- o Connect the power cables to the corresponding connectors on the graphics card. Make sure they are fully inserted and secure. Some connectors have a clip that needs to be engaged to prevent them from coming loose.

- o If your graphics card requires multiple power connectors, make sure to use separate cables from the power supply for each connector, rather than using a single cable with multiple connectors (if possible). This can help to ensure stable power delivery.

Double-Checking Your Work: Ensuring a Secure Installation

After installing the graphics card and connecting the power cables, take a moment to double-check your work:

- **Verify Full Insertion:** Ensure that the graphics card is fully seated in the PCIe slot. The retention clip should be engaged, and there should be no gaps between the card's connector and the slot.

- **Check for Sagging:** Make sure the card is level and not sagging excessively. Some larger cards may benefit from a support bracket or stand to prevent long-term stress on the PCIe slot.

- **Inspect Power Connections:** Double-check that all required power cables are securely connected to both the graphics card and the power supply.

- **Cable Management:** Use zip ties or Velcro straps to tidy up the power cables and keep them away from fans or other moving parts. Good cable management not only improves aesthetics but also helps to maintain good airflow within the case.

Post-Installation Steps: Finishing the Job

With the graphics card installed and everything double-checked, there are a few final steps to complete:

- **Reinstall the Side Panel:** If you removed your case's side panel to install the graphics card, reinstall it now.

- **Connect the Display:** Connect your monitor(s) to the appropriate ports on the graphics card using HDMI, DisplayPort, or (less commonly) DVI cables. Make sure the connections are secure.

- **Power On and Test:** Power on your system and verify that the graphics card is detected and functioning correctly. You should see the display output on your monitor(s) during the boot process.

- **Install Drivers:** Once your operating system has loaded, install the latest drivers for your graphics card. You can usually download these from the manufacturer's website (NVIDIA or AMD). Having the latest drivers ensures optimal performance and compatibility with the latest games and applications.

Troubleshooting Common Issues

While graphics card installation is usually straightforward, you may occasionally encounter issues. Here are some common problems and their potential solutions:

- **No Display Output:** If you don't see any display output after installing the graphics card, try the following:

o **Check Connections:** Make sure the monitor is properly connected to the graphics card and that the power cable is securely plugged in.

o **Reseat the Card:** Power off the system, unplug the power cable, and carefully reseat the graphics card in the PCIe slot.

o **Verify Power Connections:** Double-check that all required power cables are securely connected to the graphics card and the power supply.

o **Test with Onboard Graphics:** If your CPU has integrated graphics, try removing the graphics card and connecting your monitor to the motherboard's display output. If you get a display, the issue may be with the graphics card itself.

- **System Instability or Crashes:** If your system experiences crashes, freezes, or other stability issues after installing the graphics card, consider the following:

  o **Driver Issues:** Make sure you have the latest drivers installed for your graphics card. Try uninstalling the current drivers and performing a clean installation of the latest version.

  o **Overheating:** Monitor the temperature of your graphics card under load using monitoring software like MSI Afterburner or GPU-Z. If the card is overheating, make sure the fans are spinning and that there's adequate airflow within the case.

  o **Power Supply Issues:** In some cases, an inadequate or failing power supply can cause instability when a new graphics card is installed. Make sure your power supply meets the recommended wattage and has the necessary connectors for your card.

- **Artifacts or Glitches:** If you see visual artifacts, glitches, or other display issues, try the following:

  - o **Reseat the Card:** Power off the system and carefully reseat the graphics card.

  - o **Test with a Different Cable:** Try using a different HDMI or DisplayPort cable to connect your monitor.

  - o **Check for Driver Issues:** As with system instability, driver issues can sometimes cause visual artifacts. Try reinstalling or updating your graphics card drivers.

Upgrading Your Graphics Card in the Future

At some point, you may want to upgrade your graphics card to improve performance or take advantage of new features. The process for upgrading is similar to the initial installation:

34. **Uninstall Old Drivers:** Before removing your old graphics card, uninstall its drivers through your operating system's control panel or a utility like Display Driver Uninstaller (DDU).

35. **Power Off and Unplug:** Power off your system, unplug the power cable, and disconnect the display cables from the graphics card.

36. **Remove Old Card:** Disconnect the power cables from the graphics card, disengage the PCIe slot's retention clip, and carefully remove the card from the slot.

37. **Install New Card:** Follow the installation steps outlined earlier in this chapter to install your new graphics card.

38.   **Install New Drivers:** Once the new card is installed, power on your system and install the latest drivers for the new card.

Keep in mind that when upgrading to a significantly more powerful graphics card, you may also need to upgrade your power supply to meet the increased power requirements.

Installing a graphics card is a rewarding step in building your own PC, as it brings your system's visual capabilities to life. By carefully following the steps outlined in this chapter, you can ensure that your graphics card is properly installed, securely connected, and ready to deliver stunning visuals for all your gaming and creative needs. With your motherboard, CPU, cooler, RAM, and graphics card in place, you're nearing the final stages of your build.

CHAPTER FIFTEEN: Mounting Storage Devices

You've now installed the core components of your PC: the motherboard, CPU, CPU cooler, RAM, and graphics card. Your system is starting to take shape, but there's one crucial element missing: storage. Without storage drives, you have nowhere to install your operating system, applications, games, or personal files. In this chapter, we'll focus on mounting your storage devices, whether they are traditional hard disk drives (HDDs), solid-state drives (SSDs), or the increasingly popular NVMe SSDs.

As we discussed in Chapter 6, storage drives are your PC's long-term memory. They store data even when the power is turned off, unlike RAM which is volatile. Choosing the right type and capacity of storage is essential for a responsive and capable system. Whether you're booting up your operating system, loading a large game, or accessing your media library, the speed and capacity of your storage drives will have a significant impact on your overall experience.

Before you begin, make sure you have your storage drives readily available, along with your case manual and motherboard manual. It's also a good idea to wear your anti-static wrist strap to prevent any electrostatic discharge from damaging your components.

Understanding Storage Form Factors and Interfaces: A Quick Recap

In Chapter 6, we explored the different types of storage drives in detail. Let's quickly recap the key form factors and interfaces you're likely to encounter:

1. **3.5-inch HDDs:** These are the traditional spinning hard drives that offer large capacities at an affordable price. They are typically used for bulk storage of data that doesn't require the fastest access speeds, such as media files,

backups, and large game installations. 3.5-inch HDDs use the SATA interface, which requires both a SATA data cable and a SATA power cable.

2. **2.5-inch SATA SSDs:** These solid-state drives offer significantly faster speeds than HDDs and come in a smaller 2.5-inch form factor. They are commonly used for installing the operating system and frequently used applications to improve boot times and overall system responsiveness. Like HDDs, 2.5-inch SSDs also use the SATA interface.

3. **M.2 SATA SSDs:** These SSDs offer similar performance to 2.5-inch SATA SSDs but come in a much smaller M.2 form factor. They connect directly to an M.2 slot on the motherboard that supports the SATA interface.

4. **M.2 NVMe SSDs:** These are the fastest type of consumer storage drives, utilizing the NVMe protocol and the PCIe interface for incredibly high read and write speeds. They also use the M.2 form factor but connect to an M.2 slot that supports NVMe. NVMe SSDs are ideal for users who demand the best possible storage performance, such as gamers, content creators, and professionals working with large datasets.

It's crucial to understand the differences between these form factors and interfaces, as they determine where and how you can install your storage drives.

Mounting 3.5-inch HDDs: Installing Bulk Storage

3.5-inch HDDs are typically installed in dedicated drive bays or cages within the case. These bays are often located towards the front or bottom of the case and may be hidden behind a panel or shroud. Here's how to mount a 3.5-inch HDD:

- **Locate the 3.5-inch Drive Bays:** Consult your case manual to identify the location of the 3.5-inch drive bays.

They are usually arranged in a cage or rack and may have removable trays or tool-less mechanisms.

- **Prepare the Drive Bay:** If your case uses drive trays, remove one from the bay. Some trays require you to screw the drive into the tray, while others have a tool-less design that uses clips or pins to secure the drive.

- **Mount the Drive:** Align the HDD with the drive tray or bay, ensuring that the SATA connectors are facing the appropriate direction (usually towards the back of the case or where the cables will be routed). Secure the drive to the tray using screws if necessary, or engage the tool-less mechanism. Make sure the drive is firmly in place and doesn't wobble.

- **Slide the Tray into the Bay:** If you're using a drive tray, carefully slide it back into the drive bay until it clicks into place. If you're mounting the drive directly into the bay, align it with the mounting holes and secure it with screws.

- **Connect the Cables:** Connect one end of a SATA data cable to the SATA port on the HDD and the other end to a SATA port on the motherboard. Consult your motherboard manual to identify the SATA ports. Connect a SATA power connector from your power supply to the power port on the HDD.

Mounting 2.5-inch SATA SSDs: Adding Speed and Responsiveness

2.5-inch SATA SSDs can be mounted in various locations within the case, depending on the specific model and the available mounting options. Here are some common methods:

- **Dedicated 2.5-inch Bays:** Some cases have dedicated 2.5-inch drive bays or brackets specifically designed for SSDs. These are often located behind the motherboard tray, on the back of the 5.25-inch drive bays, or on the power supply shroud. To mount an SSD in a dedicated 2.5-inch bay, simply align the drive with the bay and secure it with screws.

- **3.5-inch Drive Trays with 2.5-inch Support:** Many 3.5-inch drive trays also have mounting holes for 2.5-inch drives. You can mount an SSD in one of these trays using the appropriate screws, and then install the tray into a 3.5-inch bay as you would with an HDD.

- **Adapter Brackets:** If your case doesn't have dedicated 2.5-inch bays or compatible drive trays, you can use a 2.5-inch to 3.5-inch adapter bracket. This allows you to mount the SSD in a standard 3.5-inch bay. Secure the SSD to the adapter bracket using screws, and then install the bracket into a 3.5-inch bay.

- **Mounting Behind the Motherboard Tray:** Some cases have mounting points behind the motherboard tray that allow you to directly attach a 2.5-inch SSD using screws. This can be a good option for keeping the SSD out of sight and maintaining a clean look.

Once you've chosen a mounting location, follow these steps to install the 2.5-inch SATA SSD:

- **Mount the SSD:** Align the SSD with the chosen mounting location and secure it using the appropriate screws. Make sure the SATA connectors are facing the direction where the cables will be routed.

- **Connect the Cables:** Connect one end of a SATA data cable to the SATA port on the SSD and the other end to a SATA port on the motherboard. Connect a SATA power connector from your power supply to the power port on the SSD.

Mounting M.2 SSDs: Embracing the Future of Storage

M.2 SSDs, whether SATA or NVMe, are installed directly into an M.2 slot on the motherboard. Here's how to mount an M.2 SSD:

- **Locate the M.2 Slot:** Consult your motherboard manual to identify the location and type of the M.2 slot(s). Most modern motherboards have at least one M.2 slot, often located near the CPU socket or the PCIe slots. Some motherboards have multiple M.2 slots, which may support different interfaces (SATA, NVMe, or both) and different lengths of M.2 drives.

- **Prepare the M.2 Slot:** If your M.2 slot has a heatsink or cover, you may need to remove it before installing the SSD. This usually involves unscrewing one or more small screws. Some motherboards also have a small screw and standoff pre-installed in the M.2 slot, which you may need to reposition depending on the length of your M.2 SSD. M.2 SSDs come in different lengths (e.g., 2280, 2260, 2242), with 2280 (80mm long) being the most common.

- **Insert the M.2 SSD:** Hold the M.2 SSD by its edges, with the connector facing downwards and the notch aligned with the key in the M.2 slot. Gently insert the SSD into the slot at a slight angle (around 20-30 degrees).

- **Secure the SSD:** Once the SSD is fully inserted, press down on the other end of the drive until it's parallel with the motherboard. Secure the SSD using the small screw that came with your motherboard. Be careful not to overtighten the screw.

- **Reinstall the Heatsink (if applicable):** If your M.2 slot has a heatsink, reinstall it over the SSD according to the motherboard manual's instructions. Some M.2 SSDs come with their own heatsinks, in which case you may not need to use the motherboard's heatsink.

Configuring Your Storage in the BIOS/UEFI: Making it Visible

After physically installing your storage drives, you may need to configure them in your system's BIOS/UEFI before they can be used by the operating system. The specific steps may vary depending on your motherboard, but here's a general overview:

39. **Enter the BIOS/UEFI:** Restart your computer and press the appropriate key during the boot process to enter the BIOS/UEFI setup. This key is usually displayed on the screen during startup and is often Del, F2, F10, or F12.

40. **Navigate to the Storage Configuration:** Look for a section in the BIOS/UEFI related to storage, SATA configuration, or NVMe configuration. The exact name and location will vary depending on your motherboard.

41. **Enable the Storage Controller(s):** Make sure that the SATA controller and/or NVMe controller is enabled. If you're using an NVMe SSD, you may also need to enable the specific M.2 slot that the drive is installed in.

42. **Set the Boot Order (Optional):** If you're installing a new operating system on one of your drives, you may need to adjust the boot order in the BIOS/UEFI to ensure that your system boots from the correct device (e.g., a USB drive or DVD containing the OS installer). You can typically find the boot order settings in a section labeled "Boot" or "Boot Priority."

43. **Save Changes and Exit:** Once you've made the necessary changes, save your settings and exit the BIOS/UEFI. Your system will restart.

Installing the Operating System: Bringing Your Storage to Life

With your storage drives installed and configured, you're ready to install your operating system. The specific steps will vary depending on the OS you're installing (e.g., Windows, Linux, macOS), but here's a general outline of the process for installing Windows:

40.   **Prepare Installation Media:** If you haven't already, create a bootable USB drive or DVD containing the Windows installation files. You can use Microsoft's Media Creation Tool to download the latest version of Windows and create the installation media.

41.   **Boot from the Installation Media:** Insert the USB drive or DVD into your computer and restart the system. Enter the BIOS/UEFI and make sure that the boot order is set to prioritize the installation media. Save changes and exit. Your system should now boot from the installation media.

42.   **Follow the On-Screen Instructions:** The Windows installer will guide you through the installation process. You'll be asked to select your language, time zone, and keyboard layout.

43.   **Choose the Installation Type:** Select "Custom: Install Windows only (advanced)" to perform a clean installation.

44.   **Select the Installation Location:** You'll be presented with a list of available storage drives. Select the drive where you want to install Windows. If the drive is new and unformatted, you may need to create a new partition by clicking "New" and specifying the desired size. For most users, it's recommended to use the entire drive for the OS partition. If you're installing Windows on an NVMe SSD, make sure to select the correct drive, as it may not be immediately obvious which one is which.

45.   **Install Windows:** Once you've selected the installation location, click "Next" to begin the installation process. Windows will copy the necessary files to the drive and install the operating system. This may take some time, and your system may restart several times during the process.

46. **Complete the Setup:** After the installation is complete, you'll be guided through the initial setup process, where you'll create a user account, set your privacy settings, and configure other preferences.

Post-Installation Steps: Finishing Touches

After installing the operating system, there are a few additional steps you should take to ensure that your storage drives are properly configured and optimized:

25. **Install Drivers:** Install the latest drivers for your motherboard, graphics card, and other components. This often includes drivers for the storage controllers, which can improve performance and compatibility. You can usually download the drivers from the manufacturers' websites or use a driver update utility.

26. **Update Firmware (SSDs):** Some SSD manufacturers offer firmware updates that can improve performance, stability, and compatibility. Check the manufacturer's website for any available firmware updates for your SSD model and follow their instructions for updating.

27. **Enable AHCI or NVMe Mode:** For SATA SSDs, make sure that the SATA controller is set to AHCI mode in the BIOS/UEFI for optimal performance. Most modern systems default to AHCI, but it's worth checking. For NVMe SSDs, ensure that the NVMe controller is enabled and that the correct drive is selected as the boot device.

28. **Optimize SSD Settings (Optional):** Some SSD manufacturers provide utility software that allows you to optimize various settings, such as over-provisioning (reserving some space for the SSD's internal management to improve performance and endurance) and enabling features like TRIM (which helps maintain performance

over time by allowing the SSD to efficiently manage deleted data).

29. **Partition and Format Additional Drives:** If you have multiple storage drives, you may need to partition and format them before you can use them to store data. In Windows, you can use the Disk Management utility to create partitions, assign drive letters, and format drives.

30. **Test Storage Performance:** To verify that your storage drives are performing as expected, you can use benchmarking utilities like CrystalDiskMark (for sequential and random read/write speeds) and AS SSD Benchmark (for access times and overall performance scores). Compare your results to reviews or other users' results with the same drive model to ensure that everything is within the expected range.

Best Practices for Managing Storage

To keep your storage drives running smoothly and efficiently, here are some best practices to follow:

31. **Regularly Defragment HDDs:** While SSDs don't require defragmentation, HDDs can benefit from periodic defragmentation to optimize file layout and improve performance. Windows has a built-in defragmentation utility that can be scheduled to run automatically.

32. **Monitor Drive Health:** Use monitoring software or your SSD's utility software to keep an eye on the health and status of your drives. Pay attention to metrics like temperature, remaining lifespan (for SSDs), and any reported errors.

33. **Enable TRIM for SSDs:** Make sure that TRIM is enabled for your SSDs to maintain performance over time. Windows typically enables TRIM automatically for supported drives, but you can verify this by running the

command `fsutil behavior query DisableDeleteNotify` in an elevated command prompt. A result of 0 means TRIM is enabled.

34. **Avoid Filling Drives to Capacity:** It's generally a good idea to leave some free space on your storage drives, especially SSDs. As drives fill up, performance can degrade, particularly write speeds. For SSDs, it's often recommended to keep at least 10-20% of the drive's capacity free.

35. **Backup Important Data:** Regularly back up your important data to an external drive, a separate internal drive, or a cloud storage service. This protects you against data loss in case of drive failure, accidental deletion, or other unforeseen events.

36. **Keep Your OS and Applications Updated:** Install the latest updates for your operating system, applications, and drivers to ensure optimal performance, compatibility, and security.

Mounting and configuring your storage drives is a crucial step in the PC building process. By carefully following the steps outlined in this chapter, you can ensure that your HDDs, SATA SSDs, and NVMe SSDs are properly installed, configured, and ready to store your data. With your storage in place, you're one step closer to completing your build.

CHAPTER SIXTEEN: Connecting the Power Supply

You've come a long way in your PC building journey. You've installed the motherboard, CPU, CPU cooler, RAM, graphics card, and storage drives. Now it's time to bring your creation to life by connecting the power supply unit (PSU), the heart of your system that will provide the vital electrical current to all your carefully selected components.

In this chapter, we'll guide you through the process of connecting your PSU to the motherboard, graphics card, storage drives, and other peripherals. This step requires careful attention to detail, as incorrect connections can potentially damage your components or prevent your system from booting. But fear not, by following the steps outlined in this chapter and consulting your PSU and motherboard manuals, you'll have your system powered up and ready to go in no time.

Before you begin, make sure your PSU is installed in your case, as covered in Chapter 7. Also, ensure that your workspace is well-lit and that you're wearing your anti-static wrist strap to prevent any electrostatic discharge from harming your components.

Understanding PSU Connectors: A Quick Recap

As we discussed in Chapter 7, your PSU comes with a variety of cables and connectors designed to power different components in your system. Let's quickly recap the most common connectors you'll be working with:

1. **24-pin ATX Connector:** This is the main power connector for the motherboard. It's a large, 24-pin connector that provides power to various components on the motherboard.

2. **4+4-pin EPS/ATX12V Connector:** This connector provides additional power to the CPU. Most modern CPUs

require an 8-pin connection, but some high-end models may need more. The 4+4-pin design allows for compatibility with both 4-pin and 8-pin sockets.

3. **6+2-pin PCIe Connector:** This connector supplies power to the graphics card. Most modern GPUs require one or more 6-pin or 8-pin PCIe connectors. The 6+2-pin design allows for compatibility with both 6-pin and 8-pin sockets.

4. **SATA Power Connector:** This connector provides power to SATA devices, such as HDDs, SSDs, and optical drives.

5. **Molex Connector:** This is an older type of connector that's less common in modern systems but may still be used for some peripherals, fans, or accessories.

It's essential to familiarize yourself with these connectors and their corresponding sockets on your components before you start connecting them.

Connecting the Motherboard: Powering the Foundation

The first step in connecting your PSU is to provide power to the motherboard. This is done using the 24-pin ATX connector and the 4+4-pin EPS/ATX12V connector.

- **Locate the 24-pin ATX Socket:** This is the largest socket on the motherboard and is usually located along the right edge. It has 24 pins arranged in a 2x12 grid.

- **Connect the 24-pin ATX Connector:** Align the 24-pin connector from your PSU with the socket on the motherboard. The connector is keyed, meaning it can only be inserted in one orientation. Gently but firmly push the connector into the socket until it clicks into place. Make sure it's fully seated and secure.

- **Locate the 4+4-pin EPS/ATX12V Socket:** This socket is usually located near the CPU socket, often towards the top-left corner of the motherboard. It may be labeled as "CPU_PWR" or something similar.

- **Connect the 4+4-pin EPS/ATX12V Connector:** If your CPU requires an 8-pin connection, combine the two 4-pin connectors from your PSU to form an 8-pin connector. Align the connector with the socket on the motherboard, ensuring that the clip on the connector aligns with the latch on the socket. Gently push the connector into the socket until it clicks into place. If your CPU only requires a 4-pin connection, use one of the 4-pin connectors and leave the other one unconnected.

Connecting the Graphics Card: Fueling Visual Performance

With the motherboard powered, it's time to connect the graphics card. As we discussed in Chapter 14, most modern graphics cards require additional power beyond what the PCIe slot can provide.

- **Identify the PCIe Power Connectors:** Locate the 6-pin or 8-pin PCIe power connectors on your graphics card. These are usually located along the top or side edge of the card. The number and type of connectors will vary depending on the specific model of your graphics card.

- **Connect the PCIe Power Cables:** Take the 6+2-pin PCIe power cables from your PSU and connect them to the corresponding sockets on the graphics card. If your card requires 8-pin connectors, combine the 6-pin and 2-pin parts of the cable to form an 8-pin connector. Align the connectors carefully and push them firmly into the sockets until they click into place. Make sure they are fully seated and secure.

- **Use Separate Cables:** If your graphics card requires multiple PCIe power connectors, it's generally recommended to use separate cables from the PSU for each connector, rather than using a single cable with multiple connectors (if possible). This can help to ensure stable power delivery and prevent overloading a single cable.

Connecting Storage Drives: Powering Your Data

Next, you'll need to connect your storage drives, whether they are HDDs, SATA SSDs, or both.

- **Locate the SATA Power Connectors:** Find the SATA power connectors on your PSU. These are flat, wide connectors with 15 pins.

- **Connect to HDDs:** For each 3.5-inch or 2.5-inch HDD, connect a SATA power connector from the PSU to the power port on the drive. The connector is keyed and can only be inserted in one orientation. Align the connector and push it firmly into the port until it's fully seated.

- **Connect to SATA SSDs:** For each 2.5-inch SATA SSD, connect a SATA power connector from the PSU to the power port on the drive. The process is the same as for HDDs.

Connecting Other Peripherals: Fans, Lighting, and More

Depending on your case and the components you've chosen, you may have other peripherals that require power connections, such as case fans, RGB lighting controllers, or fan hubs.

- **Case Fans:** Most case fans use either 3-pin or 4-pin connectors that plug directly into fan headers on the motherboard. However, some fans may use Molex connectors that connect directly to the PSU. If you have fans with Molex connectors, locate the Molex connectors on your PSU and connect them accordingly.

- **RGB Lighting:** Many modern cases and components feature RGB lighting that can be controlled through software. These often require a connection to a USB header on the motherboard for data and a SATA or Molex power connector for power. Consult the manual for your specific RGB lighting setup to determine the required connections.

- **Fan Hubs or Controllers:** If you're using a fan hub or controller to manage multiple fans, it will likely require a connection to a SATA or Molex power connector from the PSU. The individual fans will then connect to the hub or controller.

Double-Checking Your Connections: Ensuring Everything is Secure

After connecting all your components to the PSU, take some time to double-check your work:

44. **Verify All Connections:** Go through each connector you've plugged in and make sure it's fully seated and secure. Gently tug on each connector to ensure it doesn't come loose.

45. **Check for Unused Connectors:** Make sure there are no required power connectors on your components that you've missed. Consult your motherboard, graphics card, and other component manuals to verify that you've connected everything correctly.

46. **Cable Management:** Take this opportunity to tidy up your cables using zip ties or Velcro straps. Good cable management not only improves the aesthetics of your build but also helps to maintain good airflow and makes future upgrades or maintenance easier. Route the cables neatly behind the motherboard tray, through designated cable channels, and away from fans or other moving parts.

Powering On for the First Time: The Moment of Truth

With all your components connected to the PSU, it's time for the moment of truth: powering on your system for the first time.

47. **Connect the PSU to the Wall:** Plug the PSU's power cable into the back of the PSU and then into a grounded wall outlet or surge protector.

48. **Turn on the PSU:** Most PSUs have a power switch on the back. Make sure this switch is flipped to the "on" position (usually indicated by a "1" or "|").

49. **Press the Power Button:** Press the power button on the front of your case. This should send a signal to the motherboard to start the boot process.

50. **Observe the System:** Pay close attention to your system as it powers on. Look for any signs of trouble, such as sparks, smoke, or unusual noises. If you notice anything amiss, immediately turn off the system and double-check all your connections.

51. **Check for POST:** If everything is connected correctly, your system should start to POST (Power-On Self-Test). You should see lights on the motherboard and graphics card, and the fans should start spinning. If your monitor is connected, you should see the system begin to boot.

Troubleshooting Power Issues

If your system doesn't power on or if you encounter issues during the boot process, don't panic. Here are some common power-related problems and their potential solutions:

31. **No Power at All:** If nothing happens when you press the power button, try the following:

    a. **Check the PSU Switch:** Make sure the power switch on the back of the PSU is in the "on" position.

b. **Verify Wall Outlet:** Ensure that the wall outlet or surge protector you're using is working by plugging in another device.

c. **Reseat Power Connectors:** Double-check that the 24-pin ATX and 4+4-pin EPS/ATX12V connectors are fully seated on the motherboard. Also, make sure the power cable is securely connected to the PSU.

d. **Test the Power Button:** The power button on your case may be faulty or not properly connected to the motherboard. Consult your motherboard manual to locate the power switch pins on the front panel header, and try shorting them with a screwdriver to see if that powers on the system.

32. **System Powers On But No Display:** If the system seems to power on (fans spinning, lights on) but you don't see anything on your monitor, consider the following:

a. **Check Monitor Connection:** Make sure your monitor is properly connected to the graphics card (or motherboard if using integrated graphics) and that the correct input source is selected on the monitor.

b. **Reseat Graphics Card:** Power off the system and carefully reseat the graphics card in its PCIe slot. Also, double-check that all required PCIe power connectors are securely plugged in.

c. **Test with Onboard Graphics:** If your CPU has integrated graphics, try removing the graphics card and connecting your monitor to the motherboard's display output. If you get a display, the issue may be with the graphics card.

d. **Try a Different PCIe Slot:** If your motherboard has multiple PCIe x16 slots, try moving the graphics card to a different slot.

33. **System Powers On and Off Repeatedly:** If your system turns on for a few seconds and then shuts off, only to repeat the process, it could be due to:

a. **CPU Cooler Issue:** Make sure your CPU cooler is properly mounted and making good contact with the CPU. Also, ensure that the cooler's fan is connected to the CPU_FAN header on the motherboard.

b. **RAM Problem:** Try reseating your RAM modules or testing with only one module installed at a time.

c. **Short Circuit:** A loose screw or other metal object may be causing a short circuit on the motherboard. Carefully inspect the inside of your case and remove any potential culprits.

34. **System Beeps But Doesn't Boot:** If you hear a series of beeps when you power on your system, it usually indicates a specific error code. Consult your motherboard manual to determine the meaning of the beep code and troubleshoot accordingly. Common causes include RAM issues, graphics card problems, or CPU errors.

PSU Best Practices

To ensure the longevity and reliability of your PSU and the safety of your components, here are some best practices to keep in mind:

37. **Choose a Quality PSU:** As we emphasized in Chapter 7, the PSU is not a component to skimp on. Invest in a reputable brand and a model with sufficient wattage and a good efficiency rating (80 Plus Gold or higher recommended).

38.   **Don't Overload the PSU:** Make sure your PSU has enough wattage to power all your components, with some headroom for future upgrades. Use an online PSU calculator to estimate your system's power requirements.

39.   **Use the Correct Cables:** Only use the cables that came with your PSU. Don't mix and match cables from different PSUs, as the pinouts may not be compatible and could damage your components.

40.   **Maintain Good Airflow:** Ensure that your case has adequate airflow to keep the PSU and other components cool. This may involve adding additional case fans or optimizing your fan configuration.

41.   **Keep It Clean:** Over time, dust can accumulate inside the PSU, potentially affecting its performance and lifespan. Periodically clean the PSU using compressed air, but be careful not to damage any internal components. Never open the PSU casing, as this can expose you to dangerous voltages.

42.   **Consider a UPS:** An Uninterruptible Power Supply (UPS) can provide backup power to your system in the event of a power outage, allowing you to safely shut down and preventing potential data loss or hardware damage.

Connecting the power supply is a critical step in building your own PC. By carefully following the steps outlined in this chapter, double-checking your connections, and troubleshooting any issues that arise, you can ensure that your system is properly powered and ready for the next stages of the build process. With your PSU connected and your system successfully powering on, you're now ready to move on to the final steps of your PC building journey.

CHAPTER SEVENTEEN: Internal Cable Management: A Clean Build is a Happy Build

You've made it to the final stretch of the physical assembly process. Your motherboard, CPU, cooler, RAM, graphics card, storage drives, and power supply are all installed and connected. Your PC is now technically functional, but before you close up that case and call it a day, there's one more crucial step to ensure a clean, efficient, and aesthetically pleasing build: internal cable management.

Cable management is the art of organizing and routing the various cables inside your PC case in a way that minimizes clutter, maximizes airflow, and enhances the overall look of your system. While it may seem like a purely cosmetic concern, proper cable management can actually have a tangible impact on your PC's performance, longevity, and ease of maintenance.

In this chapter, we'll explore the importance of cable management and discuss various techniques and best practices for achieving a tidy and well-organized interior. We'll cover everything from planning your cable routes and using cable ties and other accessories to hiding cables behind the motherboard tray and utilizing modular power supplies. By the end of this chapter, you'll have the knowledge and skills to transform your PC's internal cabling from a tangled mess into a work of art.

Why Bother with Cable Management? The Benefits of a Clean Interior

At first glance, cable management might seem like an unnecessary step, especially if you're not planning to show off the inside of your PC. However, there are several compelling reasons to invest the time and effort into tidying up your cables:

1. **Improved Airflow:** A mess of tangled cables can obstruct airflow within the case, creating dead zones where hot air can accumulate. This can lead to higher temperatures for your components, potentially impacting performance and longevity. By routing cables neatly and keeping them out of the main airflow paths, you can ensure that your cooling system is working efficiently and that your components are getting the fresh air they need.

2. **Easier Maintenance and Upgrades:** A well-organized interior makes it much easier to access and work on your components when it comes time for maintenance or upgrades. You won't have to untangle a rat's nest of cables just to swap out a RAM module or add a new storage drive. This can save you a lot of time and frustration in the long run.

3. **Reduced Dust Buildup:** Cables can act as dust magnets, trapping dust and debris within the case. Over time, this buildup can clog fans, heatsinks, and other components, reducing their effectiveness and potentially leading to overheating. By minimizing the surface area of exposed cables and keeping them away from dust-prone areas, you can help to keep your system cleaner and reduce the frequency of maintenance.

4. **Aesthetics:** Let's face it, a clean and well-organized PC interior just looks better. Whether you have a case with a windowed side panel or not, taking pride in the craftsmanship of your build includes paying attention to the details of cable management. A tidy interior shows that you care about your system and have taken the time to do things right.

5. **Component Safety:** In extreme cases, poorly managed cables can actually pose a safety hazard to your components. Loose cables can get caught in fans, causing damage or creating noise. They can also put stress on connectors or even short-circuit if they come into contact

with the wrong parts of the motherboard or other components. Proper cable management helps to mitigate these risks.

Planning Your Cable Routes: The Key to Success

Before you start tying down cables, it's essential to have a plan. Take a moment to assess your case, components, and PSU cables to determine the best routes for each cable. Here are some factors to consider:

- **Motherboard Layout:** Familiarize yourself with the location of the various headers and connectors on your motherboard, such as the 24-pin ATX, 8-pin EPS, fan headers, front panel connectors, and SATA ports. This will help you determine the most direct and logical paths for your cables.

- **Case Features:** Examine your case for cable management features, such as:

    o **Cutouts:** Many modern cases have strategically placed cutouts in the motherboard tray that allow you to route cables behind the tray and out of sight.

    o **Grommets:** Rubber grommets around the cutouts can help to protect cables from sharp edges and provide a cleaner look.

    o **Channels:** Some cases have built-in channels or pathways for routing cables, often located behind the motherboard tray or along the edges of the case.

    o **Tie-Down Points:** Look for small loops or anchors on the back of the motherboard tray or other parts of the case. These are designed for securing cables with zip ties or Velcro straps.

- PSU Shroud: A PSU shroud is a cover that hides the power supply and its cables, creating a cleaner look in the main compartment of the case.

- **Component Placement:** Consider the location of your components, particularly the graphics card, storage drives, and any case fans. Plan your cable routes to avoid obstructing these components or interfering with their airflow.

- **PSU Cable Length:** Keep in mind the length of your PSU cables. Some cables may be longer than others, and you'll need to plan accordingly to avoid having excessive slack or cables that are too short to reach their destinations. If you're using a modular PSU, you can choose the cables you need and potentially use custom-length cables for an even cleaner look.

As you plan your cable routes, aim for the following:

- **Direct Paths:** Route cables as directly as possible from the PSU to the components, avoiding unnecessary detours or loops.

- **Hidden Cables:** Utilize the space behind the motherboard tray to hide as many cables as possible. This is where the cutouts, grommets, and channels come in handy.

- **Grouped Cables:** Bundle similar cables together using zip ties or Velcro straps. This not only looks neater but also makes it easier to manage and trace cables later on.

- **Minimal Slack:** Avoid excessive slack in your cables, as this can create clutter and obstruct airflow. However, don't make the cables too taut, as this can put stress on the connectors.

Essential Tools and Accessories: Gearing Up for Cable Management

173

While you can technically manage cables with just your hands and some patience, having the right tools and accessories can make the job much easier and more efficient. Here are some items to consider:

- **Zip Ties:** These are the most common and affordable tool for bundling and securing cables. Get a variety of sizes, from small ones for individual cables to larger ones for grouping multiple cables together. Black zip ties are generally preferred for their discreet appearance, but you can also use colored ones to color-code different cable groups.

  o Recommendation: The ঐতিন্তঢ়কিদরে Cable Ties set offers a variety of sizes.

- **Velcro Straps:** These are a reusable alternative to zip ties. They're great for cables that you may need to adjust or move frequently, such as those for external peripherals. Velcro straps come in various lengths and widths and can be easily removed and repositioned.

  o Recommendation: The ঐতিহাকিদরে Reusable Fastening Cable Straps are a good choice.

- **Cable Clips:** These small, adhesive-backed clips can be attached to the inside of your case to hold individual cables in place. They're useful for routing cables along edges or keeping them from sagging.

  o Recommendation: The ঐতিহাকিদরে Adhesive Cable Clips are well reviewed.

- **Cable Sleeves:** These are fabric or plastic tubes that you can run your cables through to create a cleaner, more uniform look. They're particularly useful for bundling multiple cables together, such as the 24-pin ATX cable. Cable sleeves come in various colors and materials to match your build's aesthetics.

o Recommendation: The ঐতিহাকিদরে Cable Management Sleeve is popular.

- **Cable Combs:** These small, comb-like accessories help to keep individual wires within a cable bundle neatly separated and parallel. They're often used with custom-sleeved cables to enhance the visual appeal of the build.

    o Recommendation: The ঐতিহাকিদরে PC Cable Combs are a good option.

- **Scissors or Wire Cutters:** You'll need a pair of scissors or flush wire cutters to trim zip ties after tightening them. Be careful not to cut the cables themselves.

- **Screwdriver:** You may need a screwdriver to remove or install components like the PSU shroud or drive cages, which can affect your cable routing options.

The Cable Management Process: Step-by-Step

With your plan in place and your tools at the ready, it's time to start managing those cables. Here's a step-by-step approach:

- **Start with the Essentials:** Begin by routing and connecting the essential power cables, such as the 24-pin ATX and the 8-pin EPS/ATX12V for the motherboard, and the PCIe power cables for the graphics card. These are usually the thickest and least flexible cables, so it's a good idea to get them in place first.

- **Route Behind the Motherboard Tray:** Whenever possible, route cables behind the motherboard tray using the cutouts and channels provided by your case. This will keep them out of sight and improve airflow in the main compartment.

- **Use Grommets:** If your case has rubber grommets around the cutouts, make sure to pass your cables through them.

This will protect the cables from sharp edges and create a cleaner look.

- **Secure with Zip Ties or Velcro Straps:** As you route your cables, secure them in place using zip ties or Velcro straps. Attach them to the tie-down points on the back of the motherboard tray or other parts of the case. Don't overtighten zip ties, as this can damage the cables. Leave a little bit of slack to allow for adjustments later on.

- **Group Similar Cables:** Bundle similar cables together, such as the SATA power cables or fan cables. This will make it easier to manage them and create a neater appearance.

- **Connect Storage Drives:** Route the SATA power and data cables to your storage drives. If possible, connect the power cables from behind the motherboard tray and the data cables from the side or bottom to minimize their visibility in the main compartment.

- **Connect Front Panel Connectors:** Route the front panel connectors (power switch, reset switch, USB, audio, etc.) to their respective headers on the motherboard. These cables are usually thin and flexible, so you can often tuck them away neatly along the edges of the case or behind the motherboard tray.

- **Manage Fan Cables:** Route your case fan cables to the appropriate fan headers on the motherboard or to a fan controller. Use zip ties or cable clips to keep them tidy and out of the way of the fan blades.

- **Address Remaining Cables:** Once all the essential cables are connected, deal with any remaining cables, such as those for RGB lighting or other accessories. Route them neatly and secure them in place.

- **Double-Check Your Work:** Before closing up your case, take a moment to double-check all your connections and make sure everything is secure. Gently tug on each cable to ensure it's properly seated in its connector.

Advanced Techniques: Taking Your Cable Management to the Next Level

If you want to go beyond the basics and achieve a truly professional-looking cable management setup, here are some advanced techniques to consider:

47. **Custom Cables:** One of the most significant upgrades you can make to your cable management is to use custom cables. These are aftermarket cables that are specifically designed for your PSU model and are often made with higher-quality materials and sleeving. Custom cables can be ordered in specific lengths and colors to perfectly match your build's aesthetics and minimize cable slack. Companies like CableMod and Ensourced offer a wide range of custom cable options.

48. **Sleeving Your Own Cables:** If you're feeling adventurous and want to save some money, you can sleeve your own PSU cables using paracord or other sleeving materials. This is a time-consuming process that requires special tools and a lot of patience, but it can result in a truly unique and customized look. There are many tutorials available online if you choose to go this route.

49. **Modifying Your Case:** For the ultimate in clean cable management, some enthusiasts resort to modifying their cases. This can involve cutting new holes or channels for cable routing, creating custom PSU shrouds or covers, or even removing or relocating drive cages. Case modification is an advanced technique that should only be attempted if you're comfortable working with tools and have a clear understanding of the potential risks involved.

50.   **Using a Modular PSU:** If you haven't already purchased your power supply, consider opting for a modular or semi-modular unit. These PSUs allow you to detach unnecessary cables, reducing clutter and making cable management much easier. With a fully modular PSU, you can use only the cables you need and leave the rest in the box.

51.   **Vertical GPU Mounting:** Some cases offer the option to mount your graphics card vertically, using a PCIe riser cable. This can create a unique look and showcase your GPU, but it also has implications for cable management. You'll need to plan your cable routes carefully to accommodate the riser cable and ensure that the GPU power cables are neatly arranged.

Maintaining Your Cable Management: Keeping it Clean

Once you've achieved a clean and well-organized cable setup, it's important to maintain it over time. Here are a few tips for keeping your cables tidy:

52.   **Periodic Cleaning:** Dust can still accumulate on and around your cables, even with good cable management. Periodically open up your case and use compressed air to remove dust from your components and cables. You can also use a soft brush or cloth to wipe down individual cables if necessary.

53.   **Adjust as Needed:** When you add, remove, or upgrade components, take the time to adjust your cable management accordingly. This may involve rerouting cables, adding or removing zip ties, or even investing in new custom cables if your needs change significantly.

54.   **Don't Rush:** When making changes to your system, resist the temptation to rush through the cable management. It's better to take your time and do it right than to end up with a messy or potentially hazardous setup.

Troubleshooting Cable Management Issues

While proper cable management is generally beneficial, there are a few potential issues to watch out for:

35. **Overtightened Zip Ties:** If you tighten zip ties too much, you can potentially damage the insulation of the cables or even crush the wires inside. Make sure to tighten zip ties just enough to secure the cables without putting excessive pressure on them.

36. **Kinked or Strained Cables:** Avoid bending cables too sharply or stretching them too taut, as this can damage the internal wires or put stress on the connectors. Aim for gentle curves and gradual transitions.

37. **Interference with Components:** Make sure your cables are not interfering with the movement of fans or other components. Also, ensure that they're not putting pressure on delicate parts of the motherboard or graphics card.

38. **Excessive Heat:** In rare cases, bundling too many cables together in a confined space can create a buildup of heat. This is more likely to be an issue with high-wattage systems or in cases with poor airflow. If you notice excessive heat around your cable bundles, consider rerouting or separating them to improve ventilation.

Cable management is an essential part of building a clean, efficient, and aesthetically pleasing PC. By planning your cable routes, using the right tools and accessories, and following the techniques outlined in this chapter, you can transform your system's interior from a tangled mess into a well-organized showcase of your building skills. Not only will your PC look better, but it will also benefit from improved airflow, easier maintenance, and potentially even enhanced performance and longevity.

CHAPTER EIGHTEEN: Installing the Operating System (OS)

You've assembled all the hardware components of your PC, and it's now a fully functional machine. However, it's still missing a crucial piece of the puzzle: the operating system (OS). The OS is the software that manages all the hardware and software resources of your computer. It provides a platform for running applications, managing files, and interacting with the hardware. Without an OS, your PC is just a collection of expensive parts.

In this chapter, we'll guide you through the process of installing an operating system on your newly built PC. While there are many operating systems available, we'll focus on the most popular choice for desktop PCs: Microsoft Windows. Specifically, we'll cover the installation of Windows 10 and Windows 11, as these are the most widely used versions at the time of writing.

Before you begin, make sure you have the following:

1. **A valid Windows license:** You'll need a valid product key to activate your copy of Windows. You can purchase a license from Microsoft or an authorized retailer.

2. **Installation media:** This can be a USB flash drive (at least 8GB) or a DVD containing the Windows installation files. You can create installation media using Microsoft's Media Creation Tool.

3. **An internet connection:** While not strictly required for the installation itself, an internet connection is necessary for downloading updates, drivers, and activating Windows.

Preparing for Installation: Backing Up and Gathering Information

Before you install a new operating system, it's essential to take a few preparatory steps:

- **Back up your data:** If you're installing Windows on a system that already has data on it, make sure to back up any important files to an external drive or cloud storage. The installation process may involve formatting the drive, which will erase all existing data.

- **Gather necessary drivers:** While Windows includes many built-in drivers, you may need to download additional drivers for specific components, such as your graphics card, network adapter, or other peripherals. It's a good idea to download these drivers beforehand and save them to a USB drive.

- **Note down your product key:** Make sure you have your Windows product key readily available. You'll need to enter it during the installation process.

- **Decide on your installation type:** You can choose between a "clean install" (which erases all existing data on the drive) or an "upgrade" (which keeps your files and settings but replaces the existing operating system). For a newly built PC, a clean install is generally recommended.

Creating Windows Installation Media: Using the Media Creation Tool

If you don't already have Windows installation media, you can create your own using Microsoft's Media Creation Tool. Here's how:

- **Download the Media Creation Tool:** Go to the official Microsoft website and download the Media Creation Tool for your desired version of Windows (Windows 10 or Windows 11).

- **Run the Tool:** Once the download is complete, run the Media Creation Tool. You'll need administrator privileges to do this.

- **Accept the License Terms:** Read and accept the license terms.

- **Choose What to Do:** Select "Create installation media (USB flash drive, DVD, or ISO file) for another PC" and click "Next."

- **Select Language, Architecture, and Edition:** The tool will automatically select the recommended options based on your current system. You can uncheck "Use the recommended options for this PC" to choose different settings if needed. Click "Next."

- **Choose Which Media to Use:** Select "USB flash drive" if you want to create a bootable USB drive, or "ISO file" if you want to create a DVD later. Click "Next."

- **Select Your USB Drive:** If you chose "USB flash drive," select your USB drive from the list. Make sure you've backed up any important data on the drive, as it will be erased. Click "Next."

- **Wait for the Process to Complete:** The Media Creation Tool will now download the Windows installation files and create the installation media. This may take some time, depending on your internet speed.

- **Finish:** Once the process is complete, click "Finish."

Booting from the Installation Media: Starting the Installation Process

With your installation media ready, you can now boot your PC from it to start the Windows installation process:

- **Insert the Installation Media:** Insert the USB drive or DVD into your PC.

- **Restart Your PC:** Restart your computer while the installation media is inserted.

- **Enter the Boot Menu:** As your PC starts up, you'll need to enter the boot menu or the BIOS/UEFI settings to change the boot order. The key to press varies depending on your motherboard, but it's often F12, F11, F8, Esc, or Del. Watch the screen during startup for a message like "Press [key] to enter boot menu" or "Press [key] for setup."

- **Select the Boot Device:** In the boot menu, you'll see a list of available boot devices. Select your USB drive or DVD drive, depending on which installation media you're using. Use the arrow keys to navigate and Enter to select.

- **Save and Exit (if in BIOS/UEFI):** If you entered the BIOS/UEFI settings instead of the boot menu, you'll need to navigate to the "Boot" or "Boot Order" section, set your installation media as the first boot device, save the changes, and exit. The exact steps vary depending on your motherboard's BIOS/UEFI.

- **Press Any Key:** Once your PC boots from the installation media, you may see a message like "Press any key to boot from USB/DVD." Press any key on your keyboard to start the Windows installation process.

Installing Windows: Step-by-Step

With your PC now booting from the installation media, you're ready to install Windows. Follow these steps:

- **Language and Preferences:** Select your language, time and currency format, and keyboard or input method. Click "Next."

- **Install Now:** Click the "Install now" button.

- **Product Key:** Enter your Windows product key when prompted. If you don't have a product key at the moment, you may be able to skip this step and enter it later. However, you won't be able to activate Windows without a valid key.

- **License Terms:** Read and accept the license terms. Click "Next."

- **Installation Type:** Choose "Custom: Install Windows only (advanced)." This option allows you to perform a clean installation and manage partitions.

- **Where to Install:** Select the drive where you want to install Windows. If the drive is new or unformatted, you'll need to create a new partition. Click "New," specify the size (or use the default to use the entire drive), and click "Apply." Windows will create the necessary system partitions.

- **Install:** Select the partition where you want to install Windows (usually "Partition 4" or "Primary") and click "Next." The installation process will now begin.

- **Wait for Installation:** Windows will copy files, install features and updates, and restart several times. This process may take a while, depending on the speed of your hardware and installation media. Do not remove the installation media during this process.

- **Set Up Your Account (Windows 10):** Once the installation is complete, you'll be guided through the initial setup process. In Windows 10, you'll be asked to:

  o Connect to a network (if available).

  o Sign in with a Microsoft account or create a local account.

- o Set up a PIN.

- o Choose privacy settings.

- o Decide whether to use Cortana.

- o Choose default apps.

- **Set Up Your Account (Windows 11):** In Windows 11, the setup process is slightly different:

  - o Select your country or region.

  - o Choose your keyboard layout.

  - o Connect to a network (if available).

  - o Name your device.

  - o Sign in with a Microsoft account (required for Windows 11 Home edition, optional for Pro edition).

  - o Set up a PIN.

  - o Choose privacy settings.

  - o Customize your experience.

  - o Decide whether to use OneDrive.

- **Wait for Final Setup:** Windows will finalize the settings and prepare your desktop. This may take a few minutes.

Post-Installation Steps: Completing the Setup

Congratulations, you've successfully installed Windows! However, there are a few more steps to complete the setup:

52.	**Install Drivers:** Windows includes many built-in drivers, but you may need to install additional drivers for optimal performance and functionality. This often includes drivers for your graphics card, network adapter, audio, and other peripherals. You can usually download the latest drivers from the manufacturers' websites or use the driver installation discs that came with your components.

53.   **Activate Windows:** To activate Windows, go to Settings > Update & Security > Activation (Windows 10) or Settings > System > Activation (Windows 11). If you entered a product key during installation, Windows might activate automatically. Otherwise, you'll need to enter your key and click "Activate."

54.   **Install Updates:** Check for and install any available Windows updates. Go to Settings > Update & Security > Windows Update (Windows 10) or Settings > Windows Update (Windows 11) and click "Check for updates." It's important to keep your system up to date for security and performance reasons.

55.   **Install Applications:** Now you can start installing your favorite applications, such as web browsers, office suites, media players, and games.

56.   **Restore Your Data:** If you backed up your data before installing Windows, you can now restore it to your newly set up system.

57.   **Personalize Your Settings:** Take some time to personalize your Windows experience. Adjust the display settings, choose a desktop background, customize the taskbar, and configure other preferences to your liking.

Troubleshooting Installation Issues

While Windows installation usually goes smoothly, you may encounter some issues along the way. Here are some common problems and their potential solutions:

55. **Installation Media Not Recognized:** If your PC doesn't boot from the installation media, double-check that you've selected the correct boot device in the BIOS/UEFI settings or boot menu. Also, make sure that the installation media was created correctly and is not corrupted.

56. **Missing Drivers During Installation:** If the Windows installer can't find your storage drive, it may be due to missing drivers. You can try loading the drivers during installation by clicking "Load driver" and browsing to the location where you saved them.

57. **Installation Freezes or Crashes:** If the installation process freezes or crashes, it could be due to hardware issues, such as faulty RAM, an unstable overclock, or overheating. Try running a memory test (e.g., MemTest86), resetting your BIOS/UEFI settings to their defaults, and ensuring that your components are adequately cooled.

58. **Activation Problems:** If you're having trouble activating Windows, double-check that you've entered the product key correctly and that you have a valid license for the edition of Windows you're installing. If you're still having issues, contact Microsoft support for assistance.

59. **Slow Installation:** If the installation process is taking an unusually long time, it could be due to slow installation media, a slow hard drive, or insufficient RAM. Make sure you're using a USB 3.0 drive if possible, and consider upgrading your storage or adding more RAM if necessary.

Dual-Booting: Installing Multiple Operating Systems

Some users may want to install multiple operating systems on the same PC, such as Windows and Linux. This is known as dual-booting. While the specific steps for setting up a dual-boot system are beyond the scope of this chapter, here are some general guidelines:

39.   **Install Windows First:** If you're planning to dual-boot with Windows and another operating system, it's generally recommended to install Windows first. This is because Windows tends to overwrite the bootloader of other operating systems, making them inaccessible.

40.   **Create a Separate Partition:** Before installing the second operating system, you'll need to create a separate partition on your storage drive. You can do this during the Windows installation process or using a disk management utility within Windows or the other OS's installer.

41.   **Install the Second OS:** Boot from the installation media of the second operating system and follow the installation process. When prompted to choose the installation location, select the partition you created earlier.

42.   **Configure the Bootloader:** After installing the second OS, you'll need to configure the bootloader to allow you to choose which operating system to boot into. Some Linux distributions, such as Ubuntu, will automatically detect the Windows installation and add it to the boot menu. In other cases, you may need to manually edit the bootloader configuration.

43.   **Set the Default OS:** You can usually set the default operating system to boot in the BIOS/UEFI settings or within the bootloader configuration.

Dual-booting can be a great way to enjoy the benefits of multiple operating systems, but it also adds complexity to your setup. Make sure you understand the process thoroughly and back up your important data before attempting to set up a dual-boot system.

CHAPTER NINETEEN: Installing Drivers and Essential Software

Your PC is assembled, the operating system is installed, and you're staring at a fresh desktop. But before you can dive into your favorite games, applications, or creative projects, there's one more crucial step: installing drivers and essential software. Drivers are the unsung heroes of your system, the software components that allow your operating system to communicate with and control your hardware. Essential software provides the basic tools and utilities you need to get the most out of your PC.

In this chapter, we'll guide you through the process of installing drivers and essential software on your newly built PC. We'll cover everything from finding and downloading the right drivers for your components to installing basic applications and utilities that every user should have. We'll also touch on some best practices for keeping your system up-to-date and running smoothly. By the end of this chapter, you'll have a fully functional and optimized system, ready to tackle any task you throw at it.

Understanding Drivers: The Language of Hardware

Think of drivers as translators between your operating system and your hardware components. Each piece of hardware in your PC, from the graphics card and network adapter to the motherboard chipset and even the mouse and keyboard, speaks its own unique language. Drivers are the software components that understand these languages and can translate them into something your operating system can understand.

Without the correct drivers, your OS wouldn't know how to communicate with your hardware, and your components either wouldn't work at all or wouldn't function properly. For example, without graphics drivers, your system might be stuck in a low-resolution mode with no 3D acceleration. Without network drivers, you wouldn't be able to connect to the internet.

Drivers are typically specific to both the hardware model and the operating system version. For example, a driver for an NVIDIA GeForce RTX 3080 graphics card on Windows 10 will be different from the driver for the same card on Windows 11 or the driver for an RTX 3070 on Windows 10.

Finding the Right Drivers: Sources and Strategies

So, how do you find the right drivers for your components? There are several sources you can turn to:

1. **Component Manufacturers' Websites:** The most reliable source for drivers is usually the website of the component manufacturer. For example, if you have an ASUS motherboard, an NVIDIA graphics card, and an Intel network adapter, you would go to the ASUS, NVIDIA, and Intel websites, respectively, to find the drivers for those specific components.

2. **Motherboard Manufacturer's Website:** For motherboard-related drivers, such as chipset, audio, and LAN drivers, the motherboard manufacturer's website is the best place to look. They often provide a comprehensive set of drivers for all the onboard components.

3. **Windows Update:** Windows includes a vast database of drivers and can often automatically detect and install drivers for many common components. While it's a convenient option, Windows Update may not always have the latest or most optimized drivers, especially for newer hardware.

4. **Driver Installation Discs:** Some components, particularly motherboards and graphics cards, may come with a driver installation disc. However, the drivers on these discs are often outdated by the time they reach users. It's generally better to download the latest drivers from the internet.

5. **Third-Party Driver Websites:** There are websites that aggregate drivers from various manufacturers. While these

can be convenient, it's crucial to exercise caution when downloading drivers from third-party sources, as they may contain malware or outdated versions. Stick to reputable sites and always scan downloaded files with an antivirus program.

When searching for drivers, it's essential to know the exact model of your components and your operating system version. You can usually find this information in your system's specifications, on the component's packaging, or by using system information tools within Windows.

Installing Drivers: A Step-by-Step Guide

The process for installing drivers can vary slightly depending on the driver and the manufacturer, but here's a general outline:

- **Download the Driver:** Go to the appropriate website (usually the component manufacturer's or motherboard manufacturer's), locate the support or downloads section, and find the driver download page for your specific component model and operating system version. Download the latest driver package.

- **Extract the Files (if necessary):** Some drivers come in a compressed format, such as a .zip or .exe file. If it's a .zip file, you'll need to extract the contents to a folder. If it's a self-extracting .exe file, you can simply run it, and it will extract the files automatically.

- **Run the Installer:** Locate the installer file, which is usually named "setup.exe," "install.exe," or something similar. Double-click the file to run the installer.

- **Follow the On-Screen Instructions:** The installer will guide you through the installation process. You may be asked to accept license agreements, choose installation options, and restart your computer. Follow the prompts carefully.

- **Restart Your PC:** After the installation is complete, it's usually necessary to restart your PC for the changes to take effect.

Special Considerations for Graphics Drivers

Graphics drivers are among the most important drivers to install, especially for gamers and users of graphically intensive applications. Here are some specific tips for installing graphics drivers:

- **Clean Installation:** Some graphics driver installers offer a "clean installation" option, which removes any previous driver versions before installing the new one. This can help to prevent conflicts or issues caused by leftover files from old drivers.

- **NVIDIA GeForce Experience and AMD Radeon Software:** NVIDIA and AMD offer software suites that can automatically detect your graphics card, download the latest drivers, and optimize game settings. These are optional but can be convenient for keeping your drivers up-to-date and getting the best performance in games.

- **Beta Drivers:** Both NVIDIA and AMD occasionally release beta drivers, which are test versions that may contain new features or performance improvements but may also be less stable than the official (WHQL-certified) drivers. Unless you're an enthusiast who wants to try out the latest features or need a fix for a specific issue, it's generally recommended to stick with the stable, certified drivers.

Installing Motherboard Drivers: Chipset, Audio, and More

Your motherboard has several onboard components that require drivers to function correctly. These often include:

- **Chipset Drivers:** These drivers manage data flow between the processor, memory, and peripherals. They are essential for optimal system performance and stability.

- **Audio Drivers:** These drivers enable your onboard audio, allowing you to hear sound through your speakers or headphones.

- **Network Drivers:** These drivers control your Ethernet and/or Wi-Fi adapter, allowing you to connect to the internet and other networks.

- **USB Drivers:** While Windows usually has built-in USB drivers, installing the motherboard's USB drivers can sometimes improve performance or enable additional features.

- **Other Drivers:** Depending on your motherboard, there may be other drivers for features like SATA controllers, Thunderbolt ports, or onboard RGB lighting.

It's generally recommended to install the chipset drivers first, followed by the other motherboard drivers. You can usually find all the necessary drivers on your motherboard manufacturer's website, in the support or downloads section for your specific motherboard model.

Installing Essential Software: Tools and Utilities

Once you've installed the necessary drivers, it's time to install some essential software that will enhance your PC experience. Here are some recommended applications and utilities:

- **Web Browser:** While Windows comes with Microsoft Edge, many users prefer to use alternative browsers like Google Chrome, Mozilla Firefox, or Opera. You can download these browsers from their respective websites.

- **Antivirus Software:** Protecting your PC from malware is crucial. Windows includes Windows Defender, which provides basic protection, but you may want to consider a more comprehensive antivirus solution from providers like Bitdefender, Norton, McAfee, or Kaspersky.

- **Office Suite:** If you need to create or edit documents, spreadsheets, or presentations, you'll need an office suite. Microsoft Office is the most popular commercial option, but there are also free alternatives like LibreOffice and OpenOffice.

- **Media Player:** To play music and videos, you can use the built-in Windows Media Player, but many users prefer more feature-rich players like VLC Media Player or Media Player Classic.

- **Compression Utility:** You'll often encounter compressed files in formats like .zip, .rar, or .7z. To extract these files, you'll need a compression utility like 7-Zip or WinRAR.

- **PDF Reader:** For viewing PDF documents, you can use the built-in PDF reader in your web browser, but a dedicated PDF reader like Adobe Acrobat Reader or Foxit Reader often provides more features.

- **System Monitoring Tools:** These tools can help you keep an eye on your system's performance, temperatures, and resource usage. Some popular options include HWMonitor, CPU-Z, GPU-Z, and MSI Afterburner.

- **Benchmarking Tools:** If you want to test your system's performance and compare it to others, you can use benchmarking tools like Cinebench (for CPU performance), 3DMark (for graphics performance), and CrystalDiskMark (for storage performance).

- **Backup Software:** It's crucial to regularly back up your important data. Windows includes a built-in backup utility, but there are also many third-party options like Macrium Reflect and EaseUS Todo Backup that offer more features and flexibility.

- **Cloud Storage:** Services like Dropbox, Google Drive, and OneDrive can be useful for syncing files across multiple devices and providing an off-site backup of your most important data.

- **Gaming Platforms:** If you're a gamer, you'll likely want to install gaming platforms like Steam, Epic Games Store, GOG Galaxy, and others to access and manage your game library.

Keeping Your System Up-to-Date: The Importance of Regular Updates

Installing drivers and software is not a one-time task. It's essential to keep your system up-to-date to ensure optimal performance, compatibility, and security. Here are some tips for maintaining your system:

58. **Enable Automatic Updates:** For your operating system and many applications, you can enable automatic updates to ensure you're always running the latest versions. In Windows, you can configure Windows Update in the Settings app.

59. **Regularly Check for Driver Updates:** Periodically check the websites of your component manufacturers for new driver releases. This is especially important for graphics drivers, as new versions often include performance improvements and optimizations for the latest games.

60. **Use Driver Update Utilities:** Some manufacturers provide utilities that can automatically detect and update drivers for their components. For example, NVIDIA

GeForce Experience and AMD Radeon Software can manage graphics driver updates.

61.   **Be Cautious with BIOS Updates:** Updating your motherboard's BIOS can sometimes improve performance, add support for new hardware, or fix bugs. However, it's a more advanced procedure that carries some risk. If your system is running stable and you don't need any specific features from a newer BIOS version, it's often best to leave it as is. If you do decide to update your BIOS, follow the manufacturer's instructions carefully and make sure you have a backup power source (like a UPS) to prevent issues in case of a power outage during the update process.

62.   **Uninstall Unused Software:** Over time, you may accumulate software that you no longer use. Periodically review your installed programs and uninstall anything you don't need. This can help to free up storage space and reduce clutter.

63.   **Perform Regular Maintenance:** Tasks like disk cleanup, disk defragmentation (for HDDs), and running antivirus scans can help to keep your system running smoothly. Windows includes built-in tools for these tasks, and there are also many third-party utilities available.

Troubleshooting Driver and Software Issues

Despite your best efforts, you may sometimes encounter issues with drivers or software. Here are some common problems and their potential solutions:

60.   **Driver Conflicts:** Occasionally, installing a new driver can conflict with an existing one, causing instability or other issues. If you experience problems after installing a new driver, try rolling back to the previous version. In Windows, you can do this through the Device Manager by right-clicking on the device, selecting "Properties," going to the "Driver" tab, and clicking "Roll Back Driver."

61. **Unsigned Drivers:** Windows prefers to use drivers that have been digitally signed by Microsoft, as this helps to ensure their compatibility and security. If you try to install an unsigned driver, you may encounter a warning or be blocked from installing it. In some cases, you may need to disable driver signature enforcement to install an unsigned driver, but this is generally not recommended unless you're sure the driver is safe.

62. **Software Compatibility Issues:** Some older software may not be fully compatible with newer versions of Windows. If you encounter issues running a particular program, try running it in compatibility mode. Right-click on the program's shortcut or executable file, select "Properties," go to the "Compatibility" tab, and check "Run this program in compatibility mode for." Then select an older version of Windows from the dropdown menu.

63. **Corrupted Installations:** Sometimes, a driver or software installation can become corrupted, leading to errors or instability. In these cases, it may be necessary to completely uninstall the driver or software and then reinstall it from scratch. For drivers, you can use the Device Manager to uninstall the device and its driver, and then reinstall the latest driver. For software, you can use the "Programs and Features" control panel to uninstall the program.

64. **System Restore:** If you encounter a serious issue after installing drivers or software, and you can't resolve it through other means, you can use Windows' System Restore feature to revert your system to an earlier state. System Restore creates restore points at regular intervals and before significant system changes, allowing you to roll back to a previous configuration if something goes wrong.

Installing drivers and essential software is a crucial step in setting up your newly built PC. By carefully selecting and installing the correct drivers for your components, you ensure that your hardware can communicate effectively with your operating system and perform at its best. By installing essential software and utilities, you equip your system with the tools you need for productivity, entertainment, and maintenance.

Remember to keep your system up-to-date by regularly checking for driver and software updates, and don't be afraid to troubleshoot if you encounter any issues. With the right drivers and software in place, your PC is now ready to provide you with a smooth, powerful, and enjoyable computing experience.

CHAPTER TWENTY: Basic BIOS/UEFI Configuration

Your PC is assembled, the operating system is installed, and your drivers and essential software are in place. You're almost ready to start using your new machine, but there's one more area to explore: the BIOS/UEFI.

The BIOS (Basic Input/Output System) or UEFI (Unified Extensible Firmware Interface) is the firmware that's built into your motherboard. It's the first software that runs when you power on your PC, and it plays a crucial role in initializing your hardware, configuring low-level settings, and booting up your operating system. While modern systems can often run fine with default BIOS/UEFI settings, understanding how to access and navigate these settings can help you troubleshoot issues, optimize performance, and unlock advanced features.

In this chapter, we'll introduce you to the basics of BIOS/UEFI configuration. We'll explain the difference between BIOS and UEFI, show you how to access the settings, and guide you through some common configuration options you may want to adjust. We'll also touch on some best practices for working with these settings and troubleshooting common issues. By the end of this chapter, you'll have a basic understanding of what the BIOS/UEFI is, what it does, and how to navigate its settings to fine-tune your PC's behavior.

BIOS vs. UEFI: Understanding the Difference

Before we dive into the settings, let's clarify the difference between BIOS and UEFI. While the terms are often used interchangeably, they represent two different approaches to firmware:

- **BIOS (Basic Input/Output System):** This is the traditional firmware that has been used in PCs since the

1980s. It's a relatively simple, text-based interface that's stored in a small ROM chip on the motherboard. BIOS has several limitations, including a 16-bit architecture, limited storage space for the firmware, and support for only MBR (Master Boot Record) partition tables, which restricts bootable drives to a maximum size of 2TB.

- **UEFI (Unified Extensible Firmware Interface):** This is the modern replacement for BIOS, introduced in the mid-2000s. UEFI is a more sophisticated firmware that offers several advantages over BIOS, including a graphical interface, mouse support, faster boot times, support for larger boot drives (using GPT, or GUID Partition Table), and enhanced security features like Secure Boot.

Most modern motherboards use UEFI, although many still include a "Legacy BIOS" or "Compatibility Support Module (CSM)" mode that allows them to boot in a BIOS-compatible way. This is useful for running older operating systems or using certain hardware that doesn't support UEFI.

Accessing the BIOS/UEFI: Entering the Setup Utility

To access the BIOS/UEFI settings, you need to enter the setup utility during the boot process. The specific key to press varies depending on your motherboard, but it's usually one of the following:

- Delete

- F2

- F1

- F10

- Esc

The key is typically displayed on the screen during the initial boot sequence, along with a message like "Press [key] to enter setup" or "[key]=Setup." You need to press the key before the operating system starts loading.

Here's how to access the BIOS/UEFI:

- Restart your PC.

- As soon as the system starts powering on, repeatedly press the appropriate key for your motherboard. It's better to press the key multiple times rather than trying to time it perfectly.

- If you've done it correctly, you should see the BIOS/UEFI setup utility appear. If the operating system starts loading instead, you've missed the window and will need to restart and try again.

Navigating the BIOS/UEFI: Using the Interface

Once you've entered the BIOS/UEFI setup utility, you'll be presented with the interface. The exact layout and options will vary depending on your motherboard, but most follow a similar structure.

UEFI interfaces are typically graphical and allow for mouse input, while older BIOS interfaces are usually text-based and require keyboard navigation. Here are some common navigation controls:

- **Arrow keys:** Used to move between menus, options, and fields.

- **Enter:** Used to select a menu or option, or to confirm a change.

- **Esc:** Usually used to go back to the previous menu or to discard changes.

- **+/- keys:** Often used to change values or cycle through options.

- **F1:** Typically displays help information.

- **F10:** Usually the key to save changes and exit.

The BIOS/UEFI interface is typically divided into several sections or menus, each containing related settings. Common sections include:

- **Main:** Provides basic system information, such as the date, time, and installed hardware.

- **Advanced:** Contains settings for various onboard devices, such as the CPU, chipset, storage, and USB.

- **Boot:** Allows you to configure the boot order and other boot-related settings.

- **Security:** Contains settings related to passwords, Secure Boot, and other security features.

- **Power:** Allows you to configure power management settings.

- **Overclocking (OC):** If your motherboard supports overclocking, this section will contain settings for adjusting CPU and memory frequencies, voltages, and timings.

- **Tools:** May include utilities for updating the BIOS/UEFI, managing fan profiles, or configuring RAID.

Common BIOS/UEFI Settings: Tweaking Your System

While the specific settings available in your BIOS/UEFI will depend on your motherboard, here are some common options you may want to configure:

64. **Boot Order:** This setting determines the order in which your system checks for bootable devices when it starts up. You can configure it to boot from a specific hard drive, SSD, USB drive, or optical drive. To install an

operating system from a USB drive or DVD, you'll need to set the appropriate device as the first boot option.

65. **XMP/DOCP:** As we discussed in Chapter 13, XMP (Extreme Memory Profile) and DOCP (Direct Over Clock Profile) are settings that allow your RAM to run at its rated speed and timings. Enabling XMP/DOCP can improve memory performance, especially if you've purchased high-speed RAM. This setting is usually found in the overclocking or memory settings section.

66. **SATA Mode:** This setting determines how your SATA controller operates. The most common options are:

   a. **IDE:** An older compatibility mode that's generally slower and not recommended for modern systems.

   b. **AHCI:** The standard mode for SATA devices, offering better performance and features like Native Command Queuing (NCQ). This is the recommended setting for most users.

   c. **RAID:** Allows you to combine multiple drives into a RAID array for improved performance, redundancy, or both. This is a more advanced configuration that requires specific knowledge and setup.

67. **Secure Boot:** This is a UEFI feature that helps to prevent unauthorized code from running during the boot process, enhancing system security. It works by verifying the digital signatures of bootloaders and other critical software components. Secure Boot is enabled by default on most modern systems, but you may need to disable it to boot from certain older operating systems or use specific hardware.

68. **Virtualization:** If you plan to use virtualization software like VMware or VirtualBox, you'll need to enable virtualization support in the BIOS/UEFI. This setting is

often called "Intel Virtualization Technology" (Intel VT-x) or "AMD Virtualization" (AMD-V) and is usually found in the CPU or chipset settings.

69.   **Onboard Devices:** The BIOS/UEFI allows you to enable or disable various onboard devices, such as the integrated graphics, audio, network adapter, or USB ports. If you're not using a particular device, disabling it can free up system resources and potentially improve boot times.

70.   **Fan Control:** Many modern motherboards offer fan control settings in the BIOS/UEFI, allowing you to adjust fan curves and set temperature thresholds. This can help you balance cooling performance and noise levels.

71.   **Date and Time:** It's important to set the correct date and time in the BIOS/UEFI, as this information is used by the operating system for various purposes, such as file timestamps and scheduled tasks.

Saving Changes and Exiting: Applying Your Configuration

After making changes to the BIOS/UEFI settings, you'll need to save them and exit the setup utility. Here's how:

65.   **Save Changes:** Look for an option labeled "Save Changes and Reset," "Save Changes and Exit," or something similar. This is often assigned to the F10 key, but it may vary depending on your motherboard. Selecting this option will save your changes to the CMOS memory and restart the system.

66.   **Discard Changes:** If you've made changes that you don't want to keep, look for an option labeled "Discard Changes and Exit" or "Exit Without Saving." This will exit the setup utility without saving any changes.

67.   **Load Defaults:** If you've made changes that have caused issues or if you want to revert to the default settings, look for an option labeled "Load Optimized

Defaults," "Load Setup Defaults," or something similar. This will reset all settings to their factory defaults. Be aware that this will also reset any customizations you've made, such as your boot order or XMP profile.

Updating the BIOS/UEFI: Keeping Your Firmware Current

Occasionally, motherboard manufacturers release updates to the BIOS/UEFI firmware. These updates can provide various benefits, such as:

44.   Improved hardware compatibility (e.g., support for new CPUs or RAM)

45.   Performance enhancements

46.   Bug fixes

47.   Security updates

While it's not always necessary to update to the latest BIOS/UEFI version, it's generally a good idea to do so if the update addresses a specific issue you're experiencing or if it provides important security or compatibility improvements.

Here's a general overview of how to update the BIOS/UEFI:

43.   **Identify Your Motherboard Model and Current BIOS/UEFI Version:** You can usually find this information in the BIOS/UEFI setup utility itself, in the system information section. Alternatively, you can use system information tools within Windows, such as CPU-Z or the System Information utility.

44.   **Download the Update:** Go to your motherboard manufacturer's website and find the support or downloads section for your specific motherboard model. Look for the latest BIOS/UEFI update and download it. Make sure to read any release notes or instructions provided with the update.

45. **Prepare a USB Drive:** Most modern motherboards allow you to update the BIOS/UEFI from a USB drive. You'll need a USB drive formatted with the FAT32 file system. Copy the downloaded BIOS/UEFI update file to the root directory of the USB drive.

46. **Enter the BIOS/UEFI Setup Utility:** Restart your PC and enter the BIOS/UEFI setup utility as described earlier.

47. **Use the Update Utility:** Look for a built-in utility for updating the BIOS/UEFI. This is often called "EZ Flash," "Q-Flash," "M-Flash," or something similar, depending on the motherboard brand. It's usually found in the "Tools" or "Advanced" section.

48. **Select the Update File:** Use the update utility to select the BIOS/UEFI update file from your USB drive.

49. **Start the Update Process:** Follow the on-screen instructions to start the update process. This may involve confirming that you want to proceed and verifying the file's integrity.

50. **Do Not Interrupt the Update:** It's crucial not to interrupt the update process once it has started. Do not power off or restart your PC, even if it seems like nothing is happening. Interrupting the update can potentially corrupt the BIOS/UEFI, rendering your motherboard unusable.

51. **Wait for Completion:** The update process may take several minutes. Once it's complete, your system will usually restart automatically.

52. **Verify the Update:** After the system restarts, enter the BIOS/UEFI setup utility again and verify that the new version has been successfully installed.

It's important to note that updating the BIOS/UEFI carries some risk. If something goes wrong during the update process, such as a power outage or a corrupted update file, it can potentially "brick" your motherboard, making it unbootable. To minimize the risk:

23.   Make sure you have a stable power source. If possible, use an Uninterruptible Power Supply (UPS) to prevent power interruptions during the update.

24.   Double-check that you've downloaded the correct update file for your specific motherboard model.

25.   Carefully follow the instructions provided by your motherboard manufacturer.

26.   Don't update the BIOS/UEFI unless you have a specific reason to do so. If your system is running fine and you don't need any of the features or fixes provided by the update, it's often best to leave it as is.

Troubleshooting BIOS/UEFI Issues

While most BIOS/UEFI interactions are trouble-free, you may occasionally encounter issues. Here are some common problems and their potential solutions:

3. **System Won't POST:** If your system fails to complete the Power-On Self-Test (POST) and you don't see any display output, it could be due to a BIOS/UEFI issue. Try the following:

    o **Clear CMOS:** Clearing the CMOS memory can reset the BIOS/UEFI settings to their defaults, which may resolve compatibility issues or incorrect settings. Most motherboards have a dedicated jumper or button for clearing the CMOS. Consult your motherboard manual for the specific procedure. Alternatively, you can remove the CMOS battery for a few minutes.

- o **Check for Beep Codes:** If your system emits a series of beeps during startup, these may indicate a specific error code. Consult your motherboard manual to interpret the beep codes and identify the potential issue.

- o **Reseat Components:** Try reseating your RAM, graphics card, and other components to ensure they're making proper contact.

- o **Test with Minimal Hardware:** Disconnect any non-essential hardware, such as extra storage drives, expansion cards, and peripherals. Try to boot with just the CPU, one RAM module, and integrated graphics (if available) to rule out issues with other components.

4. **Incorrect Settings:** If you've made changes to the BIOS/UEFI settings and are experiencing issues, try the following:

- o **Load Defaults:** Use the "Load Optimized Defaults" or similar option in the BIOS/UEFI to reset all settings to their factory defaults.

- o **Revert Specific Changes:** If you know which specific setting is causing the problem, try reverting that setting to its previous value.

5. **Boot Order Problems:** If your system is not booting from the correct device, double-check the boot order settings in the BIOS/UEFI. Make sure the desired boot device is listed first.

6. **Compatibility Issues:** If you've recently installed new hardware and are experiencing issues, it could be due to a compatibility problem. Check the motherboard manufacturer's website for any BIOS/UEFI updates that may address compatibility issues with your specific hardware.

7. **Failed BIOS/UEFI Update:** If your system becomes unbootable after a failed BIOS/UEFI update, you may need to use a recovery method, if available. Some motherboards have a dual BIOS feature that allows you to switch to a backup BIOS in case the primary one becomes corrupted. Others may have a USB BIOS flashback feature that allows you to update the BIOS/UEFI using a USB drive without needing a working CPU or RAM. Consult your motherboard manual for any available recovery options. In the worst case, you may need to use an external programmer to reflash the BIOS/UEFI chip or replace the motherboard.

The BIOS/UEFI is a critical component of your PC, providing the low-level interface between your hardware and operating system. By understanding how to access and navigate the BIOS/UEFI settings, you can fine-tune your system's behavior, optimize performance, and troubleshoot issues. Remember to exercise caution when making changes to these settings, as incorrect configurations can potentially cause instability or even prevent your system from booting. Always consult your motherboard manual for specific instructions and information, and don't be afraid to load the default settings if you run into trouble.

With your BIOS/UEFI configured and your system booting correctly, you've reached a major milestone in your PC building journey. In the next chapter, we'll cover the final steps of testing and troubleshooting your build to ensure everything is running smoothly before you start using your new PC for work or play.

CHAPTER TWENTY-ONE: Testing and Troubleshooting Your Build

You've meticulously assembled your PC, installed the operating system, drivers, and essential software, and configured your BIOS/UEFI settings. Now comes the moment of truth: verifying that everything works as expected and troubleshooting any issues that may arise. This crucial phase, known as testing and troubleshooting, ensures that your newly built PC is stable, performs optimally, and is ready for everyday use.

In this chapter, we'll guide you through the process of testing your PC's hardware and software, covering various techniques and tools for evaluating system stability, performance, and functionality. We'll also delve into common troubleshooting scenarios, providing you with practical solutions to diagnose and resolve issues that may occur during the initial testing phase or later on. By the end of this chapter, you'll have the knowledge and skills to thoroughly test your build, identify and fix any problems, and ensure that your PC is running smoothly and reliably.

Initial Power-On and POST: The First Signs of Life

The first step in testing your build is to power it on and observe the initial boot process. This is known as the Power-On Self-Test (POST), during which the BIOS/UEFI initializes the hardware and checks for any critical errors.

1. **Connect Peripherals:** Connect your monitor, keyboard, and mouse to the appropriate ports on your PC.

2. **Power On:** Press the power button on your case.

3. **Observe the POST:** Pay close attention to the system's behavior during the POST. You should see lights on the motherboard and graphics card, and fans should start

spinning. Your monitor should display the motherboard manufacturer's logo or some initial text output.

4. **Listen for Beep Codes:** In some cases, the system may emit a series of beeps during POST. These beep codes can indicate specific errors, such as a problem with the RAM or graphics card. Consult your motherboard manual to interpret any beep codes you hear.

5. **Enter BIOS/UEFI (Optional):** If you want to verify your hardware configuration or make any final adjustments, you can enter the BIOS/UEFI settings by pressing the appropriate key during POST (usually Del, F2, F1, F10, or Esc).

If your system successfully completes the POST and boots into the operating system, that's a great sign! It means that the essential hardware components are functioning and communicating properly. However, if you encounter any issues during POST, such as no display output, unusual beeps, or the system powering off immediately, refer to the troubleshooting sections in previous chapters (particularly Chapters 16, 18, and 20) or consult your motherboard manual for specific guidance.

Verifying Hardware Detection: Ensuring Everything is Recognized

Once your system has booted into the operating system, the next step is to verify that all your hardware components are detected and functioning correctly.

- **Device Manager (Windows):** In Windows, open the Device Manager by right-clicking the Start button and selecting "Device Manager." This utility provides a hierarchical view of all the hardware installed in your system.

- **Check for Unknown Devices:** Look for any devices with a yellow exclamation mark or a red "X" icon. These indicate that the device is not recognized or has a driver issue. If you find any unknown devices, right-click on them and select "Update driver" to try and automatically install the correct driver. If that doesn't work, you may need to manually download and install the driver from the component manufacturer's website.

- **Verify Component Details:** Expand each category in the Device Manager and check that all your components are listed correctly. For example, under "Display adapters," you should see your graphics card model; under "Disk drives," you should see your installed storage drives; under "Processors," you should see your CPU model and the number of cores.

- **System Information:** You can also use the System Information utility to get a detailed overview of your hardware configuration. Press the Windows key, type "msinfo32," and press Enter to open it. This utility provides information about your CPU, RAM, motherboard, graphics card, storage, and other components.

Stress Testing: Pushing Your System to the Limit

After verifying that all your hardware is detected, it's time to put your system through its paces with stress testing. Stress testing involves running demanding software that pushes your components to their maximum capacity for an extended period. This helps to ensure that your system is stable under heavy load and that your cooling solution is adequate.

Several popular tools can be used for stress testing:

- **Prime95:** This is a widely used utility for stress-testing CPUs. It runs complex mathematical calculations that put a heavy load on the processor, testing its stability and temperature. Download the latest version from the official website, extract the files, and run "prime95.exe." Select the "Just Stress Testing" option and choose the "Small FFTs" test for maximum heat generation. Let the test run for at least several hours, or even overnight, while monitoring your CPU temperatures.

- **MemTest86:** This is a memory testing utility that can help identify errors or instability in your RAM. Download the utility, create a bootable USB drive, and boot from it. The test will run automatically and should be allowed to complete at least one full pass, which can take several hours depending on the amount of RAM you have.

- **FurMark:** This is a GPU stress-testing utility that renders complex 3D scenes to push your graphics card to its limits. Download the latest version from the official website, install it, and run the "GPU stress test." Monitor your GPU temperatures and watch for any visual artifacts or crashes.

- **Heaven Benchmark/Valley Benchmark:** These are two popular benchmarks from Unigine that can also be used for stress testing. They render beautiful and demanding 3D scenes that put a heavy load on both the CPU and GPU. Download the benchmarks from the official website, install them, and run them in a loop for several hours.

- **AIDA64:** This is a comprehensive system information and diagnostic tool that also includes a stability test. The stability test can stress test the CPU, GPU, RAM, and storage simultaneously. AIDA64 is a commercial product, but a trial version is available.

While running stress tests, it's crucial to monitor your system's temperatures using monitoring software like HWMonitor, Core Temp, or the utilities provided by your motherboard or graphics card manufacturer. Keep an eye on the following:

- **CPU Temperature:** Most modern CPUs can handle temperatures up to around 90-95°C under heavy load, but it's generally recommended to keep them below 80-85°C for optimal longevity and stability.

- **GPU Temperature:** Graphics cards can typically run a bit hotter than CPUs, with some models reaching up to 80-90°C under load. However, it's a good idea to keep them below 80°C if possible.

- **VRM Temperature:** The Voltage Regulator Modules (VRMs) on the motherboard can also get hot, especially during CPU stress testing. While they're designed to handle high temperatures, it's generally a good idea to keep them below 100°C.

- **RAM Temperature:** RAM typically doesn't generate as much heat as the CPU or GPU, but it's still worth monitoring, especially if you're overclocking or using high-performance modules.

If you observe excessively high temperatures during stress testing, you may need to improve your cooling solution, adjust your fan curves, or reapply thermal paste. If your system crashes, freezes, or shows other signs of instability during stress testing, it could indicate a problem with your hardware, drivers, or BIOS/UEFI settings.

Performance Benchmarking: Measuring Your PC's Capabilities

Benchmarking is the process of running standardized tests to measure your PC's performance in various tasks, such as gaming, content creation, and general computing. Benchmarks can help you:

- Compare your PC's performance to other systems

- Identify performance bottlenecks

- Verify the effectiveness of overclocking or other tweaks

- Ensure that your system is performing as expected for its specifications

Here are some popular benchmarking tools:

72.   **Cinebench:** This benchmark measures CPU performance by rendering a complex 3D scene. It provides a score for both single-core and multi-core performance. Cinebench is useful for evaluating your CPU's capabilities in content creation tasks like video editing and 3D rendering.

73.   **3DMark:** This is a suite of benchmarks designed to test gaming performance. It includes various tests that simulate different gaming scenarios and resolutions. 3DMark provides scores for overall performance, graphics, and physics, allowing you to compare your system to others and see how well it can handle modern games.

74.   **Unigine Heaven/Valley/Superposition:** These benchmarks render beautiful and demanding 3D scenes to test your system's graphics performance. They provide detailed performance metrics, including FPS (frames per second), frame times, and GPU temperature.

75.   **PCMark:** This is a comprehensive benchmark that tests overall system performance in a variety of real-world tasks, such as web browsing, video conferencing, photo editing, and document creation. PCMark provides an overall score as well as individual scores for different workloads.

76.   **CrystalDiskMark:** This benchmark measures the read and write speeds of your storage drives. It provides sequential and random access performance metrics, allowing you to evaluate the speed of your SSDs and HDDs.

77.   **UserBenchmark:** This is a free, all-in-one benchmark that tests your CPU, GPU, RAM, and storage. It provides an easy-to-understand report that compares

your system's performance to other users with the same components.

When running benchmarks, it's important to:

68. Close any unnecessary background applications to ensure accurate results.

69. Run the benchmark multiple times and take the average score to account for any variability.

70. Compare your results to those of similar systems to see if your performance is in line with expectations.

71. Use the same settings and resolution when comparing results across different systems or configurations.

Real-World Testing: Using Your PC as Intended

While stress tests and benchmarks are useful for evaluating system stability and performance under controlled conditions, it's also important to test your PC in real-world scenarios that reflect your actual usage.

48. **Gaming:** If you built your PC for gaming, spend some time playing your favorite games at your desired settings and resolution. Monitor your frame rates (using tools like MSI Afterburner or the game's built-in FPS counter) and watch for any stutters, freezes, or visual artifacts.

49. **Content Creation:** If you plan to use your PC for tasks like video editing, 3D modeling, or photo editing, try running your usual software and working on some projects. Pay attention to rendering times, responsiveness, and any signs of instability.

50. **General Use:** Use your PC for everyday tasks like web browsing, email, office applications, and media

playback. Make sure everything feels smooth and responsive, and that you don't encounter any unexpected issues.

During real-world testing, keep an eye on your system's temperatures and listen for any unusual noises, such as excessive fan noise, coil whine, or clicking sounds from hard drives. These could indicate potential issues that need to be addressed.

Troubleshooting Common Issues: Solving Problems Methodically

Despite your best efforts, you may encounter issues during the testing and troubleshooting phase. Here's a systematic approach to diagnosing and resolving common problems:

53.   **Identify the Symptoms:** Pay close attention to the specific symptoms you're experiencing. When does the issue occur (e.g., during startup, under heavy load, after a certain period of time)? Are there any error messages or unusual behaviors?

54.   **Isolate the Cause:** Try to narrow down the potential causes of the issue by considering what has changed recently (e.g., new hardware, drivers, or software) and what specific actions or conditions trigger the problem.

55.   **Consult Online Resources:** Search online forums, communities, and support websites for users who may have experienced similar issues. Look for solutions or workarounds that have been successful for others.

56.   **Check Event Viewer (Windows):** The Event Viewer is a Windows utility that logs system events, errors, and warnings. It can provide valuable clues about the cause of crashes, freezes, and other issues. To access the Event Viewer, press the Windows key, type "eventvwr," and press Enter. Look for any critical errors or warnings around the time the problem occurred.

57.   **Test Individual Components:** If you suspect a particular component is causing the issue, try to test it in isolation. For example, you can test your RAM using MemTest86, your CPU using Prime95, and your GPU using FurMark. You can also try swapping out components with known working ones, if available, to see if the problem persists.

58.   **Update or Roll Back Drivers:** Driver issues can often cause instability or performance problems. Try updating to the latest drivers for your components, or if you recently updated drivers, try rolling back to a previous version.

59.   **Check BIOS/UEFI Settings:** Incorrect BIOS/UEFI settings can sometimes cause issues. If you've made changes to the settings, try reverting to the default settings or adjusting individual settings one at a time to see if it resolves the problem.

60.   **Reinstall the Operating System:** If you've ruled out hardware issues and suspect a software or driver problem, you can try reinstalling the operating system as a last resort. Make sure to back up any important data before doing this.

Long-Term Monitoring and Maintenance: Keeping Your System Healthy

Once you've thoroughly tested your system and resolved any issues, it's important to continue monitoring its performance and health over time. Here are some tips for long-term maintenance:

27.   **Regularly Monitor Temperatures:** Keep an eye on your CPU and GPU temperatures, especially during demanding tasks like gaming or content creation. Use monitoring software to track temperatures over time and watch for any significant increases that could indicate a problem with your cooling system.

28. **Clean Your System:** Dust buildup can negatively impact cooling performance and potentially cause issues over time. Periodically open up your case and use compressed air to remove dust from fans, heatsinks, and other components. Clean your case's dust filters regularly.

29. **Update Drivers and Software:** Stay up-to-date with the latest drivers for your components and the latest versions of your essential software. Check the manufacturers' websites periodically or use driver update utilities.

30. **Monitor Storage Health:** Keep an eye on the health of your storage drives using monitoring tools or the utilities provided by the drive manufacturer. Look for any signs of errors or degradation, and replace drives as needed.

31. **Run Periodic Stress Tests:** It's a good idea to run stress tests occasionally, especially after making hardware or software changes, to ensure that your system remains stable under heavy load.

32. **Back Up Your Data:** Regularly back up your important data to an external drive or cloud storage. This will protect you against data loss in case of hardware failure, software issues, or other unforeseen events.

Testing and troubleshooting are essential steps in the PC building process. By thoroughly testing your system's stability, performance, and functionality, you can ensure that your newly built PC is running at its best and is ready for any task you throw at it. Remember to be patient and methodical when diagnosing and resolving issues, and don't be afraid to seek help from online communities or the manufacturers of your components.

With your PC fully tested and optimized, you've completed the challenging but rewarding journey of building your own computer. You now have a custom-built machine that meets your specific needs and preferences, and you've gained valuable knowledge and experience that will serve you well in future upgrades and builds.

CHAPTER TWENTY-TWO:
Overclocking: Risks and Rewards (Optional)

You've built your PC, installed the operating system, drivers, and essential software, and thoroughly tested your system for stability and performance. You're now enjoying the fruits of your labor, but you might be wondering if there's a way to squeeze even more performance out of your carefully selected components. That's where overclocking comes in.

Overclocking is the process of running a component, typically the CPU or GPU, at a higher clock speed than the manufacturer's specified rating. By increasing the frequency at which the component operates, you can potentially achieve higher performance in games, content creation applications, and other demanding tasks. However, overclocking is not without its risks and complexities. It requires careful tweaking, thorough testing, and a good understanding of the underlying hardware.

In this chapter, we'll explore the world of overclocking, covering the potential benefits and risks, the basic principles involved, and the tools and techniques used to push your hardware beyond its stock settings. We'll focus primarily on CPU and GPU overclocking, as these are the most common and impactful types of overclocking for most users. We'll also touch on RAM overclocking and discuss some of the precautions you need to take to avoid damaging your components. By the end of this chapter, you'll have a basic understanding of what overclocking is, how it works, and whether it's something you want to pursue with your own PC.

The Allure of Overclocking: Why Push Your Hardware Further?

Before we dive into the technical details, let's discuss why people overclock their components in the first place. The primary motivation is usually to achieve higher performance without spending more money on new hardware. By overclocking your existing CPU or GPU, you may be able to:

1. **Improve Gaming Performance:** In games that are CPU or GPU-bound, overclocking can increase your frame rates, providing a smoother and more responsive gaming experience. This can be particularly noticeable in older games or at lower resolutions, where the CPU is more likely to be a bottleneck.

2. **Boost Productivity:** In content creation applications like video editing, 3D rendering, and photo editing, overclocking can reduce the time it takes to complete tasks. A faster CPU can encode video or render scenes more quickly, while a faster GPU can accelerate tasks like video playback and photo manipulation.

3. **Extend the Lifespan of Your Hardware:** Overclocking can help you keep up with the demands of new software without having to upgrade your components as frequently. By pushing your existing hardware further, you may be able to delay the need for a costly upgrade.

4. **Bragging Rights:** For some enthusiasts, overclocking is a hobby in itself. It's a way to push the limits of their hardware and compete with other overclockers to achieve the highest possible clock speeds or benchmark scores.

The Risks of Overclocking: Proceed with Caution

While overclocking can offer significant benefits, it's essential to understand the potential risks involved:

- **Increased Heat Output:** Running a component at a higher clock speed typically requires increasing its voltage, which in turn generates more heat. If your cooling system is not adequate, this can lead to overheating, which can cause instability, throttling, or even permanent damage to the component.

- **Reduced Lifespan:** Higher voltages and temperatures can accelerate the degradation of the components over time, potentially shortening their lifespan. While moderate overclocking with proper cooling is unlikely to cause immediate damage, it may reduce the longevity of your CPU or GPU.

- **System Instability:** Overclocking can introduce instability if the settings are too aggressive or if the component is not capable of running reliably at the higher speeds. This can manifest as crashes, freezes, blue screens, or other unpredictable behavior.

- **Voiding Warranties:** Most manufacturers state that overclocking voids the warranty of their products. If you damage your CPU or GPU while overclocking, you may not be able to get it repaired or replaced under warranty.

- **Time and Effort:** Overclocking requires a significant investment of time and effort. It involves a lot of trial and error, testing, and tweaking to find the optimal settings for your specific hardware.

Overclocking Basics: Understanding the Principles

To understand how overclocking works, let's briefly review some key concepts:

- **Clock Speed:** This is the frequency at which a component operates, measured in gigahertz (GHz). It determines how many cycles or operations the component can perform per second. A higher clock speed generally means faster performance.

- **Voltage:** This is the electrical potential supplied to the component. Increasing the voltage can help to stabilize a component at higher clock speeds, but it also increases power consumption and heat output.

- **Multiplier:** The CPU multiplier, also known as the clock ratio, determines the relationship between the base clock (BCLK) and the final CPU clock speed. For example, if the BCLK is 100 MHz and the multiplier is 45, the CPU clock speed will be 4.5 GHz (100 MHz * 45).

- **Base Clock (BCLK):** This is the base frequency of the motherboard, measured in megahertz (MHz). It's used as a reference for various other clocks in the system, including the CPU, memory, and PCIe. On most modern Intel systems, the BCLK is fixed at 100 MHz, and overclocking is primarily done by adjusting the multiplier. However, some platforms allow for BCLK adjustments, which can provide more fine-grained control but can also affect the stability of other components.

- **Cooling:** As mentioned earlier, cooling is crucial for overclocking. The better your cooling solution, the more headroom you'll have for increasing clock speeds and voltages.

CPU Overclocking: Pushing the Processor

CPU overclocking is typically done through the BIOS/UEFI, although some motherboard manufacturers provide software utilities that allow for overclocking within the operating system. The basic process involves:

- **Entering the BIOS/UEFI:** Restart your PC and enter the BIOS/UEFI setup by pressing the appropriate key during startup (usually Del, F2, or Esc).

- **Locating Overclocking Settings:** Find the section related to overclocking or CPU settings. This is often labeled "OC," "Ai Tweaker," "Extreme Tweaker," or something similar, depending on your motherboard brand.

- **Adjusting the Multiplier:** The simplest way to overclock most modern CPUs is to increase the multiplier. Start by increasing the multiplier by one step (e.g., from 45x to 46x) and saving the changes.

- **Testing for Stability:** Boot into your operating system and run a stress test, such as Prime95, to check for stability. Monitor CPU temperatures to ensure they stay within safe limits.

- **Increasing Voltage (if necessary):** If the system is unstable or crashes during the stress test, you may need to increase the CPU voltage. This is usually done in small increments (e.g., 0.01V or 0.025V). Be cautious when increasing voltage, as excessive voltage can damage the CPU.

- **Repeating the Process:** Continue increasing the multiplier and/or voltage, testing for stability after each change, until you reach the desired clock speed or encounter instability that cannot be resolved with reasonable voltage adjustments.

- **Fine-Tuning:** Once you've found a stable overclock, you can try fine-tuning the settings to find the lowest possible voltage that maintains stability. This can help to reduce heat output and power consumption.

It's important to note that not all CPUs are equally overclockable. Some chips may be able to reach much higher clock speeds than others, even within the same model line. This is due to variations in the manufacturing process, known as the "silicon lottery." Additionally, some CPUs, particularly Intel's non-K series and most AMD CPUs, have locked multipliers that prevent or limit overclocking.

GPU Overclocking: Unleashing Graphics Potential

GPU overclocking is typically done using software utilities provided by the graphics card manufacturer or third-party tools like MSI Afterburner. The process involves:

- **Installing Overclocking Software:** Download and install a GPU overclocking utility, such as MSI Afterburner, EVGA Precision X1, or ASUS GPU Tweak.

- **Increasing Core Clock:** Use the software to gradually increase the GPU core clock speed in small increments (e.g., 10-20 MHz).

- **Testing for Stability:** Run a graphics benchmark or stress test, such as Unigine Heaven or FurMark, to check for stability and watch for visual artifacts or crashes.

- **Increasing Memory Clock:** Once you've found a stable core clock, you can start increasing the memory clock speed, also in small increments.

- **Adjusting Voltage (Optional):** Some overclocking utilities allow you to adjust the GPU voltage. This can help to stabilize higher clock speeds but also significantly increases heat output and power consumption. Use caution when adjusting GPU voltage.

- **Fine-Tuning:** As with CPU overclocking, you can try to find the lowest possible voltage that maintains stability at your desired clock speeds.

- **Saving Profiles:** Most overclocking utilities allow you to save your settings as profiles, so you can easily switch between different clock speeds and voltages depending on your needs.

When overclocking your GPU, pay close attention to temperatures and fan speeds. Make sure your graphics card has adequate cooling to handle the increased heat output.

RAM Overclocking: Speeding Up Memory

RAM overclocking involves increasing the frequency and/or tightening the timings of your memory modules beyond their stock specifications. This can provide a performance boost in memory-intensive applications and can also help to improve CPU performance, especially on platforms like AMD's Ryzen, which are more sensitive to memory speed.

RAM overclocking can be done either through the BIOS/UEFI or using software utilities within the operating system. The process typically involves:

78. **Enabling XMP/DOCP:** As we discussed in Chapter 13, XMP and DOCP are pre-defined profiles that automatically configure your RAM to run at its rated speed and timings. This is the easiest way to overclock your RAM and is a good starting point for further tweaking.

79. **Manually Adjusting Frequency:** If you want to push your RAM beyond its XMP/DOCP settings, you can manually increase the frequency in the BIOS/UEFI. Start with small increments (e.g., 100-200 MHz) and test for stability after each change.

80. **Adjusting Timings:** RAM timings determine the latency of various memory operations. Lower timings generally result in better performance, but they can also affect stability. You can try tightening the primary timings (tCL, tRCD, tRP, tRAS) one at a time, testing for stability after each change.

81. **Increasing Voltage:** If you encounter instability, you may need to increase the DRAM voltage. Most DDR4 RAM can handle up to 1.35-1.45V, while DDR5 typically operates at around 1.1-1.3V. Consult your RAM's specifications and be cautious when increasing voltage, as excessive voltage can damage the modules.

82.   **Testing for Stability:** Use a memory stress test like MemTest86 to check for stability after each change. Run the test for at least several hours to ensure there are no errors.

RAM overclocking can be quite complex and time-consuming, as there are many different timings and settings to tweak. It's often best to start with XMP/DOCP and then experiment with small adjustments to see if you can further improve performance.

Cooling and Power Considerations: Keeping It Cool and Stable

As mentioned earlier, cooling is crucial when overclocking. Here are some tips for keeping your components cool:

72.   **Upgrade Your Cooler:** If you're planning to do significant overclocking, consider upgrading to a more powerful CPU cooler. For air coolers, look for models with larger heatsinks and multiple fans. For liquid cooling, consider an AIO with a 240mm or larger radiator.

73.   **Improve Case Airflow:** Make sure your case has adequate airflow, with intake fans bringing in cool air and exhaust fans expelling hot air. You may need to add more fans or upgrade to higher-airflow models.

74.   **Monitor Temperatures:** Use monitoring software to keep an eye on your CPU, GPU, and VRM temperatures, especially during stress testing. Make sure they stay within safe limits.

75.   **Consider a More Powerful PSU:** Overclocking increases power consumption, so make sure your power supply has enough wattage to handle the increased load. It's a good idea to have at least a 100-200W headroom above your system's estimated power consumption when overclocking.

76. **Use High-Quality Thermal Paste:** When installing your CPU cooler, use a high-quality thermal paste to ensure optimal heat transfer between the CPU and the cooler.

Testing for Stability: Ensuring Reliability

Stability testing is a critical part of the overclocking process. It's essential to thoroughly test your system after each change to ensure that it remains stable under load. Here are some tips for stability testing:

51. **Use Multiple Stress Tests:** Don't rely on a single stress test. Use a combination of CPU, GPU, and memory stress tests to ensure that all components are stable.

52. **Run Tests for Extended Periods:** Stability issues may not always show up immediately. Run stress tests for at least several hours, or even overnight, to ensure that your system can handle sustained loads.

53. **Monitor for Errors:** Pay attention to any errors, crashes, or unusual behavior during stress testing. If you encounter any issues, dial back your overclock settings and retest.

54. **Test in Real-World Scenarios:** In addition to synthetic stress tests, also test your system in real-world applications that you use regularly, such as games or content creation software.

55. **Keep a Log:** Keep a record of your overclock settings, including frequencies, voltages, and temperatures. This will help you track your progress and identify any patterns or issues.

The Downside of Overclocking: Potential Drawbacks

While overclocking can be a rewarding experience, it's important to be aware of the potential downsides:

61. **Time Commitment:** Overclocking can be a time-consuming process, requiring a lot of trial and error, testing, and tweaking.

62. **Steep Learning Curve:** Understanding the various settings and their interactions can be challenging, especially for beginners.

63. **Risk of Damage:** While modern hardware has built-in protections against damage from over-voltage and over-temperature conditions, there's always a risk that pushing components too far can cause permanent damage.

64. **Diminishing Returns:** As you increase clock speeds, the performance gains often become smaller while the heat output and power consumption increase significantly. There's usually a "sweet spot" beyond which further overclocking yields minimal benefits.

65. **System Instability:** Even if your system appears stable during stress testing, you may still encounter occasional crashes or instability in certain applications or scenarios.

Alternatives to Overclocking: Other Ways to Boost Performance

If you're not comfortable with the risks or complexity of overclocking, there are other ways to improve your PC's performance:

33. **Upgrade Your Components:** The most straightforward way to boost performance is to upgrade to faster hardware, such as a newer CPU, GPU, or SSD.

34. **Optimize Your Software:** Make sure your operating system, drivers, and applications are up to date. Uninstall any unnecessary software and disable any startup programs that you don't need.

35.   **Add More RAM:** If your system is running low on memory, adding more RAM can improve performance, especially in multitasking scenarios.

36.   **Enable XMP/DOCP:** As mentioned earlier, enabling XMP/DOCP is an easy way to boost memory performance without manually overclocking.

37.   **Use SSDs:** If you're still using a traditional hard drive, upgrading to an SSD can dramatically improve system responsiveness and loading times.

38.   **Clean Your System:** Regularly cleaning the dust out of your PC and ensuring proper airflow can help maintain optimal performance.

Overclocking can be a fun and rewarding way to push your PC's performance beyond its stock settings. However, it's not for everyone, and it's essential to understand the risks and complexities involved before you begin. By carefully researching and following the guidelines outlined in this chapter, you can safely experiment with overclocking and potentially achieve significant performance gains. Remember to start with small adjustments, thoroughly test for stability, and monitor your temperatures closely. And if you're not comfortable with the risks or don't have the time to invest in the process, don't worry – there are plenty of other ways to optimize your PC's performance. Ultimately, the most important thing is to build a system that meets your needs and provides a stable and enjoyable computing experience.

CHAPTER TWENTY-THREE:
Peripherals: Choosing Keyboards, Mice, and Monitors

You've built your PC, installed the operating system, drivers, and essential software, and even dabbled in the art of overclocking. Your machine is humming along beautifully, but there's one crucial aspect we haven't discussed yet: how you'll actually interact with this powerful creation. That's where peripherals come in - the devices that allow you to input commands, view output, and generally experience your PC's capabilities.

In this chapter, we'll focus on three of the most essential peripherals: keyboards, mice, and monitors. These are the primary tools you'll use to control your PC, and choosing the right ones can significantly impact your overall computing experience, whether you're gaming, working, or simply browsing the web. We'll explore the different types of keyboards and mice available, discuss the key features to consider when choosing a monitor, and provide some recommendations to help you make informed decisions. By the end of this chapter, you'll have a solid understanding of what to look for in these essential peripherals and be ready to complete your setup with the perfect input and display devices.

Keyboards: The Foundation of Input

The keyboard is your primary tool for text input, navigation, and issuing commands to your PC. While it might seem like a simple device, there's a surprising amount of variety in the world of keyboards. Choosing the right one can make a big difference in your typing comfort, speed, and overall experience.

Mechanical vs. Membrane: The Great Keyboard Divide

One of the most fundamental distinctions in keyboards is the type of switch they use:

1. **Membrane Keyboards:** These keyboards use a layer of rubber or silicone membranes beneath the keys. When you press a key, it pushes down on the membrane, completing a circuit and registering the keystroke. Membrane keyboards are typically the most affordable option and are often found in budget-oriented pre-built PCs and laptops.

   o **Pros:** Affordable, quiet, often spill-resistant.

   o **Cons:** Mushy feel, less tactile feedback, shorter lifespan.

2. **Mechanical Keyboards:** These keyboards use individual mechanical switches under each key. Each switch contains a physical mechanism, usually involving a spring and metal contacts, that registers the keystroke. Mechanical keyboards are favored by many enthusiasts and professionals for their responsiveness, durability, and satisfying feel.

   o **Pros:** Tactile feedback, faster response times, longer lifespan, customizable.

   o **Cons:** More expensive, can be noisier, larger footprint.

Mechanical Switches: A World of Options

If you opt for a mechanical keyboard, you'll encounter a wide variety of switch types, each with its own unique characteristics. Switches are often categorized by their "color," which denotes their feel and sound. Here are some of the most common types:

- **Linear Switches (e.g., Cherry MX Red, Gateron Red):** These switches have a smooth, consistent feel throughout the keypress, with no tactile bump or click. They're often preferred by gamers for their fast and responsive action.

- **Tactile Switches (e.g., Cherry MX Brown, Gateron Brown):** These switches have a noticeable bump partway through the keypress, providing tactile feedback that lets you know the key has been registered. They're a popular choice for typing and general use.

- **Clicky Switches (e.g., Cherry MX Blue, Gateron Blue):** These switches have both a tactile bump and an audible click when actuated. They provide the most feedback but can be quite noisy, making them less suitable for shared workspaces.

In addition to these main categories, there are also many variations and specialized switches available, such as silent switches, speed switches, and low-profile switches. Some manufacturers even offer optical switches, which use light sensors instead of physical contacts to register keystrokes, potentially offering even faster response times and longer lifespans.

Keycaps: Material and Printing

The keycaps, the plastic covers that sit on top of the switches, also play a role in the typing experience. They come in various materials and printing methods:

- **ABS Plastic:** This is the most common keycap material. It's relatively inexpensive but can develop a shiny or greasy appearance over time with heavy use.

- **PBT Plastic:** This is a more durable and higher-quality plastic that's resistant to shine and wear. PBT keycaps often have a slightly textured feel.

- **Doubleshot Molding:** This is a manufacturing process where two separate pieces of plastic are molded together to create the keycap legend (the letter or symbol on the key). Doubleshot keycaps are very durable, as the legends won't fade or wear off over time.

- **Dye Sublimation:** This is a printing method where the dye is infused into the plastic of the keycap. Dye-sublimated legends are also very durable and resistant to wear.

- **Laser Etching:** This is a common method for creating legends on keycaps, especially on backlit keyboards. The legend is etched into the keycap using a laser. Laser-etched legends can sometimes wear off over time, depending on the quality of the etching and the keycap material.

Form Factors: Size and Layout

Keyboards come in various sizes and layouts, often referred to as form factors. Here are some common ones:

- **Full-Size:** This is the standard keyboard layout, typically featuring 104 keys, including a numeric keypad.

- **Tenkeyless (TKL):** This layout omits the numeric keypad, resulting in a more compact size. It's a popular choice for gamers and users who want to save desk space.

- **75%:** This layout is even more compact than TKL, further reducing the space between keys and often omitting some less frequently used keys like Scroll Lock and Pause.

- **60%:** This is a minimalist layout that omits the function row, arrow keys, and navigation cluster, in addition to the numeric keypad. 60% keyboards often use function layers to access the missing keys.

- **Split and Ergonomic:** These keyboards are designed to reduce strain and promote a more natural typing posture. They may feature a split layout, angled key clusters, or built-in wrist rests.

Connectivity: Wired vs. Wireless

Keyboards can connect to your PC via either a wired or wireless connection:

- **Wired:** Wired keyboards typically connect via USB. They offer a reliable connection with no input lag, making them the preferred choice for gaming and other latency-sensitive applications.

- **Wireless:** Wireless keyboards can connect via Bluetooth or a 2.4 GHz wireless receiver (usually a small USB dongle). They offer more freedom of movement and reduce cable clutter but can be slightly more expensive and may introduce a small amount of input lag.

Additional Features: Backlighting, Macros, and More

Many keyboards offer additional features that can enhance your experience:

83. **Backlighting:** Backlit keyboards have LEDs that illuminate the keys, making them easier to see in low-light conditions. Some keyboards offer single-color backlighting, while others feature full RGB lighting with customizable colors and effects.

84. **Macro Keys:** Macro keys are programmable keys that can be assigned to perform specific actions or sequences of actions. They can be useful for automating repetitive tasks or executing complex commands in games.

85. **Media Controls:** Some keyboards have dedicated media keys or knobs for controlling volume, playback, and other media functions.

86. **USB Passthrough:** A USB passthrough port allows you to connect a USB device, such as a mouse or flash drive, directly to the keyboard, which can be convenient for reducing cable clutter or accessing a port more easily.

87. **Wrist Rests:** A wrist rest can provide support and improve comfort during long typing sessions. Some keyboards come with detachable wrist rests, while others have integrated ones.

Mice: Precision Pointing

The mouse is your primary tool for navigating graphical interfaces, selecting objects, and interacting with applications. Like keyboards, mice come in various shapes, sizes, and designs, with different features catering to different needs and preferences.

Sensor Types: Optical vs. Laser

The heart of a mouse is its sensor, which tracks the mouse's movement across a surface. There are two main types of mouse sensors:

77. **Optical Sensors:** These sensors use an LED to illuminate the surface beneath the mouse and a small camera to capture images of the surface. The mouse's processor then analyzes these images to determine the direction and speed of movement. Optical sensors are generally accurate and work well on a variety of surfaces, especially mouse pads.

78. **Laser Sensors:** These sensors use a laser instead of an LED to illuminate the surface. Laser sensors can track on a wider range of surfaces, including glossy or reflective ones, but they can sometimes be overly sensitive or exhibit "acceleration" issues, where the cursor moves faster than expected based on the mouse's movement.

For most users, the difference between optical and laser sensors is negligible. However, gamers often prefer optical sensors for their consistent and predictable tracking.

DPI/CPI: Sensitivity and Precision

DPI (dots per inch) or CPI (counts per inch) is a measure of a mouse's sensitivity. It determines how many pixels the cursor will move on the screen for every inch you move the mouse. A higher DPI means the cursor will move farther with less physical movement.

Many modern mice allow you to adjust the DPI on the fly, either through dedicated buttons or software. This can be useful for switching between different tasks that require varying levels of precision. For example, you might use a lower DPI for precise aiming in a first-person shooter game and a higher DPI for general web browsing.

Ergonomics: Shape, Size, and Grip Style

The shape and size of a mouse can significantly impact its comfort and usability. Mice come in various designs, from ambidextrous models that can be used by both left- and right-handed users to ergonomically shaped mice that are designed to fit the natural contours of your hand.

Your grip style also plays a role in choosing the right mouse. There are three main grip styles:

56.   **Palm Grip:** The most common grip style, where your entire hand rests on the mouse. Palm grip users often prefer larger, more sculpted mice.

57.   **Claw Grip:** A grip style where your palm rests on the back of the mouse, and your fingers are arched to click the buttons. Claw grip users may prefer smaller, lighter mice.

58.   **Fingertip Grip:** A grip style where only your fingertips are in contact with the mouse. Fingertip grip users often prefer small, lightweight mice that can be easily moved with just the fingers.

Connectivity: Wired vs. Wireless

Like keyboards, mice can be either wired or wireless:

66.   **Wired:** Wired mice typically connect via USB and offer a reliable, lag-free connection. They are generally preferred by gamers and users who require the most responsive and consistent performance.

67.   **Wireless:** Wireless mice can connect via Bluetooth or a 2.4 GHz wireless receiver. They offer more freedom of movement and reduce cable clutter but may introduce a small amount of input lag and require periodic battery replacement or recharging.

Additional Features: Buttons, Scroll Wheels, and More

Modern mice often come with additional features that can enhance their functionality:

39.   **Extra Buttons:** Many mice have additional buttons beyond the standard left and right clicks, such as side buttons, DPI adjustment buttons, or even small joysticks. These buttons can be programmed to perform various actions or macros.

40.   **Scroll Wheel:** The scroll wheel is used for vertical scrolling and can often be clicked as an additional button. Some mice also offer horizontal scrolling or "tilt-wheel" functionality.

41.   **Adjustable Weight:** Some gaming mice come with removable weights that allow you to customize the mouse's weight and balance to your preference.

42.   **RGB Lighting:** Like many PC components these days, some mice feature RGB lighting that can be customized to match your system's aesthetics.

43.   **Onboard Memory:** Some mice have onboard memory that allows you to save your settings, such as DPI levels and button assignments, directly to the mouse. This means you can use your preferred settings on any PC without having to reinstall software or reconfigure the mouse.

Monitors: The Window to Your PC

The monitor is your primary visual output device, displaying everything from your operating system's desktop to your favorite games and movies. Choosing the right monitor can make a big difference in your overall computing experience, affecting everything from image quality and color accuracy to responsiveness and eye comfort.

Panel Types: TN, IPS, and VA

Monitors use different types of LCD (Liquid Crystal Display) panels, each with its own strengths and weaknesses:

8. **TN (Twisted Nematic):** TN panels are the oldest and most affordable LCD technology. They offer fast response times and high refresh rates, making them popular among gamers. However, they typically have narrower viewing angles and less accurate color reproduction compared to other panel types.

9. **IPS (In-Plane Switching):** IPS panels are known for their wide viewing angles and accurate colors, making them a good choice for content creators and users who value image quality. They generally have slower response times than TN panels, but advancements in technology have narrowed the gap in recent years.

10. **VA (Vertical Alignment):** VA panels offer a good balance between TN and IPS, with better contrast ratios and deeper blacks than either. They have wider viewing angles than TN but not as wide as IPS. Response times are typically slower than TN but faster than IPS.

Resolution: Pixel Count Matters

Resolution refers to the number of pixels on the screen, typically expressed as width × height. Higher resolutions offer more screen real estate and sharper images but also require more graphics processing power. Common resolutions include:

8. **1080p (1920×1080):** Also known as Full HD, this is the most common resolution for entry-level and mainstream monitors.

9. **1440p (2560×1440):** Also known as QHD or 2K, this resolution offers a good balance between image quality and performance requirements. It's becoming increasingly popular for gaming and general use.

10.   **4K (3840×2160):** Also known as Ultra HD or UHD, this resolution provides incredibly sharp and detailed images but requires a powerful graphics card to drive, especially for gaming.

11.   **Ultrawide:** Ultrawide monitors have aspect ratios wider than the standard 16:9, such as 21:9 or 32:9. They offer more horizontal screen space, which can be useful for multitasking, immersive gaming, and content creation. Common ultrawide resolutions include 2560×1080, 3440×1440, and 5120×1440.

Refresh Rate: Smooth Motion

Refresh rate, measured in Hertz (Hz), refers to the number of times per second the monitor updates the image on the screen. A higher refresh rate results in smoother motion, which can be particularly beneficial for gaming. While most standard monitors have a refresh rate of 60Hz, gaming monitors often offer refresh rates of 144Hz, 240Hz, or even higher.

To take full advantage of a high refresh rate monitor, your graphics card needs to be capable of rendering games at a correspondingly high frame rate. For example, to fully utilize a 144Hz monitor, you'll want your games to run at 144 frames per second (FPS) or higher.

Response Time: Avoiding Ghosting

Response time refers to the time it takes for a pixel to change from one color to another. A faster response time results in less motion blur or "ghosting" in fast-paced scenes. Response times are typically measured in milliseconds (ms).

For gaming, a response time of 5ms or lower is generally recommended. Some gaming monitors advertise response times as low as 1ms, but it's important to note that these figures can sometimes be misleading, as they may refer to the best-case scenario rather than the average performance.

Adaptive Sync: Eliminating Screen Tearing

Screen tearing is a visual artifact that occurs when the graphics card's output is not in sync with the monitor's refresh rate. It results in a horizontal "tear" across the screen, where two different frames are displayed at the same time.

Adaptive sync technologies, such as AMD FreeSync and NVIDIA G-SYNC, help to eliminate screen tearing by synchronizing the monitor's refresh rate to the graphics card's output. This results in a smoother, more fluid gaming experience.

7. **AMD FreeSync:** This is an open standard that works with AMD graphics cards and is supported by many monitor manufacturers. FreeSync monitors are typically more affordable than G-SYNC monitors.

8. **NVIDIA G-SYNC:** This is a proprietary technology that requires a special hardware module in the monitor. G-SYNC monitors tend to be more expensive but often offer better performance and additional features. G-SYNC works with NVIDIA graphics cards.

9. **G-SYNC Compatible:** In recent years, NVIDIA has started certifying some FreeSync monitors as "G-SYNC Compatible." These monitors don't have the dedicated G-SYNC hardware module but have been tested and validated by NVIDIA to provide a good variable refresh rate experience with NVIDIA graphics cards.

HDR: High Dynamic Range

High Dynamic Range (HDR) is a technology that allows for a wider range of brightness and color than standard dynamic range (SDR). HDR content can display brighter highlights, darker shadows, and more vibrant colors, resulting in a more realistic and immersive image.

To enjoy HDR content, you need both an HDR-capable monitor and HDR content. There are several HDR standards, including HDR10, HDR10+, Dolby Vision, and HLG. When choosing an HDR monitor, pay attention to its peak brightness (measured in nits or cd/m²) and its color gamut coverage.

Connectivity: Ports and Inputs

Monitors offer various connectivity options for connecting to your PC and other devices:

- **HDMI:** The most common digital interface for connecting to PCs, gaming consoles, and other devices. HDMI supports both video and audio.

- **DisplayPort:** Another digital interface that's commonly used for connecting to PCs. DisplayPort often offers higher bandwidth than HDMI, making it suitable for high-resolution, high-refresh-rate monitors.

- **USB-C:** Some modern monitors offer USB-C connectivity, which can carry video, audio, data, and power over a single cable. This is particularly useful for connecting to laptops that support USB-C video output.

- **Legacy Ports:** Some monitors may still include older analog ports like VGA or DVI, but these are becoming increasingly rare and are generally not recommended for modern systems.

When choosing a monitor, make sure it has the necessary ports to connect to your PC's graphics card and any other devices you plan to use.

Ergonomics: Adjustability and Comfort

Monitor ergonomics are important for maintaining a comfortable and healthy posture during long computing sessions. Look for monitors that offer:

- **Height Adjustment:** The ability to adjust the monitor's height allows you to position the top of the screen at or slightly below eye level, which is generally recommended for optimal ergonomics.

- **Tilt Adjustment:** The ability to tilt the screen forward and backward helps you find the most comfortable viewing angle and reduce glare.

- **Swivel Adjustment:** Some monitors allow you to swivel the screen left and right, which can be useful for sharing the screen with others or adjusting your viewing position.

- **Pivot Adjustment:** The ability to rotate the screen 90 degrees into portrait mode can be useful for certain tasks like reading long documents or coding.

- **VESA Mount Compatibility:** VESA mount compatibility allows you to attach the monitor to a third-party stand or arm, providing even more flexibility in positioning and ergonomics. Look for monitors that support the common 100x100mm or 75x75mm VESA mount standards.

Other Features: Built-in Speakers, USB Hubs, and More

Some monitors offer additional features that can enhance your experience:

- **Built-in Speakers:** While built-in monitor speakers are typically not as good as dedicated external speakers or headphones, they can be convenient for casual use or if you want to minimize desk clutter.

- **USB Hub:** A built-in USB hub allows you to connect USB devices directly to the monitor, which can be useful for cable management or if your PC is located far from your desk.

- **KVM Switch:** Some high-end monitors include a built-in KVM (Keyboard, Video, Mouse) switch, which allows you to control multiple PCs with a single set of peripherals.

- **Picture-in-Picture (PIP) and Picture-by-Picture (PBP):** These features allow you to display multiple input sources on the screen simultaneously, which can be useful for multitasking or monitoring multiple systems.

Choosing the Right Peripherals for Your Needs

With so many options available, choosing the right keyboard, mouse, and monitor can seem overwhelming. Here's a step-by-step approach to help you make informed decisions:

- **Determine Your Budget:** Peripherals can range widely in price, from budget-friendly options to high-end models with advanced features. Set a budget for each peripheral before you start shopping.

- **Consider Your Usage:** Think about how you plan to use your PC. Are you a gamer, a content creator, an office worker, or a casual user? Different usage scenarios may prioritize different features.

- **Research and Read Reviews:** Look for reviews and recommendations from reputable sources, such as tech websites, YouTube channels, and user forums. Pay attention to both expert reviews and user feedback.

- **Try Before You Buy (If Possible):** If you have the opportunity, try out different keyboards and mice in person at a local electronics store. This can give you a better sense of their feel and ergonomics.

- **Prioritize Key Features:** Based on your usage and preferences, prioritize the features that are most important to you. For example, if you're a gamer, you might prioritize a mechanical keyboard with fast switches, a mouse with a high-DPI optical sensor, and a monitor with a high refresh rate and low response time.

- **Consider the Ecosystem:** If you're investing in multiple peripherals from the same brand, you may benefit from a unified software ecosystem that allows you to control settings and synchronize RGB lighting across all your devices.

- **Don't Forget the Basics:** While it's tempting to focus on the most advanced features, don't overlook the basics like comfort, durability, and ease of use. A peripheral that looks great on paper but feels uncomfortable or awkward in practice won't do you much good.

Conclusion

Choosing the right peripherals is a crucial part of setting up your PC. Your keyboard, mouse, and monitor are the primary tools you'll use to interact with your system, and they can significantly impact your overall computing experience. By understanding the different types of peripherals available, the key features to consider, and your own specific needs and preferences, you can make informed decisions that will enhance your productivity, gaming performance, and enjoyment of your new PC.

Remember that there's no one-size-fits-all solution when it comes to peripherals. What works best for one user may not be ideal for another. Take your time, do your research, and choose the peripherals that best suit your individual requirements and budget. With the right keyboard, mouse, and monitor, you'll be well-equipped to take full advantage of your powerful new PC and enjoy a comfortable, immersive, and productive computing experience.

CHAPTER TWENTY-FOUR: Upgrading Your PC in the Future

You've built your PC, installed the operating system, drivers, and software, and you're enjoying the fruits of your labor. But the journey doesn't end here. One of the great advantages of building your own PC is the ability to upgrade individual components over time, extending the lifespan of your system and keeping up with the ever-evolving demands of software and games.

In this chapter, we'll explore the world of PC upgrades. We'll discuss the reasons why you might want to upgrade, how to identify which components to upgrade first, and the process of installing and configuring new hardware. We'll also touch on some considerations for future-proofing your system and making smart upgrade choices that provide the best value and performance. By the end of this chapter, you'll have a solid understanding of how to approach upgrades and ensure that your PC remains powerful and relevant for years to come.

Why Upgrade? Recognizing the Need for Change

Technology moves fast, and the PC you built today may not meet your needs forever. Here are some common reasons why you might consider upgrading your PC:

1. **Performance Bottlenecks:** Over time, you may notice that your PC is no longer keeping up with the latest software or games. Certain components may become bottlenecks, limiting the overall performance of your system. For example, an older graphics card may struggle to run new games at your desired settings, or a lack of RAM can cause slowdowns when multitasking.

2. **New Technologies:** The PC industry is constantly evolving, with new technologies and standards emerging regularly. You may want to upgrade to take advantage of

new features, such as faster storage interfaces (e.g., NVMe SSDs), new graphics card architectures, or improved connectivity options (e.g., USB 4, Wi-Fi 6E).

3. **Changing Needs:** Your computing needs may change over time. For example, you might start pursuing a new hobby like video editing or 3D modeling that requires more powerful hardware. Or, you may find yourself working with larger datasets or more demanding applications that push your current system to its limits.

4. **Component Failure:** Unfortunately, hardware components can fail over time. While some failures are sudden and catastrophic, others may manifest as gradual performance degradation or intermittent issues. Upgrading can be an opportunity to replace failing components and improve overall system reliability.

5. **The Itch to Tinker:** For some PC enthusiasts, upgrading is a hobby in itself. The desire to experiment with new hardware, optimize performance, and keep up with the latest technology can be a driving force behind upgrades, even if they're not strictly necessary.

Identifying Upgrade Priorities: Targeting the Weak Links

Before you start buying new components, it's important to identify which parts of your system are most in need of an upgrade. Here's a step-by-step approach to help you prioritize:

- **Monitor System Performance:** Use monitoring tools like Task Manager, Resource Monitor, or third-party utilities like HWMonitor or MSI Afterburner to observe your system's behavior under load. Pay attention to CPU usage, GPU usage, RAM usage, and disk activity.

- **Identify Bottlenecks:** Look for components that are consistently running at or near 100% utilization while others are not being fully utilized. This can indicate a bottleneck. For example, if your CPU is constantly at 100% usage during gaming while your GPU is only at 60%, your CPU is likely the bottleneck.

- **Consider Your Usage:** Think about the specific tasks or applications where you're experiencing performance issues. Are you struggling with slow frame rates in games? Long render times in video editing software? Sluggish multitasking? This can help you pinpoint which components to upgrade.

- **Research Common Upgrade Paths:** Look online for recommendations and benchmarks based on your current hardware and your performance goals. Websites, forums, and YouTube channels dedicated to PC hardware can provide valuable insights into which upgrades are likely to provide the biggest improvements for your specific system.

- **Set a Budget:** Determine how much you're willing to spend on upgrades. This will help you narrow down your options and make informed decisions about which components to prioritize.

Common Upgrade Paths: Where to Focus Your Efforts

While every system is different, here are some common upgrade paths that often provide significant performance improvements:

- **Graphics Card (GPU):** For gamers, the graphics card is usually the most impactful component for improving frame rates and visual fidelity. Upgrading to a newer, more powerful GPU can often provide a substantial boost in gaming performance.

- **Solid-State Drive (SSD):** If your system is still using a traditional hard disk drive (HDD) as its primary storage, upgrading to an SSD is one of the most noticeable improvements you can make. SSDs offer drastically faster boot times, application loading times, and overall system responsiveness. If you already have a SATA SSD, consider upgrading to a faster NVMe SSD if your motherboard supports it.

- **RAM:** If you're running low on RAM, adding more can improve multitasking performance and reduce slowdowns caused by swapping data to the slower storage drive. For most users, 16GB is a good minimum, while 32GB or more may be beneficial for demanding applications or heavy multitasking.

- **CPU:** Upgrading the CPU can provide a boost in both gaming and productivity tasks, especially if your current CPU is several generations old or is a lower-end model. However, CPU upgrades often require a motherboard upgrade as well, which can be a more involved and costly process.

- **Monitor:** While not a direct performance upgrade, a higher-resolution, higher-refresh-rate, or larger monitor can significantly enhance your visual experience, particularly for gaming and content creation.

- **Power Supply (PSU):** If you're upgrading to more power-hungry components, such as a high-end graphics card or a more powerful CPU, you may need to upgrade your PSU to ensure it can provide enough stable power.

Performing Upgrades: A Step-by-Step Guide

Once you've identified the components you want to upgrade, it's time to get your hands dirty. The specific steps for each component will vary, but here's a general overview of the upgrade process:

- **Backup Your Data:** Before making any hardware changes, it's crucial to back up your important data. This is especially important if you're upgrading storage drives or reinstalling the operating system.

- **Research Compatibility:** Ensure that the new components you've chosen are compatible with your existing hardware, particularly your motherboard. Check the motherboard manufacturer's website for CPU and RAM compatibility lists, and make sure your case and power supply can accommodate the new components.

- **Prepare Your Workspace:** Gather all the necessary tools, such as screwdrivers, anti-static wrist strap, and zip ties. Make sure your workspace is clean, well-lit, and static-free.

- **Power Down and Unplug:** Turn off your PC, switch off the power supply, and unplug the power cable from the wall outlet.

- **Ground Yourself:** Wear an anti-static wrist strap and connect it to an unpainted metal part of the case to prevent electrostatic discharge from damaging your components.

- **Remove Existing Components:** Carefully remove the components you're replacing, following the reverse of the installation procedures outlined in previous chapters. For example, to remove a graphics card, you'll need to disconnect the PCIe power cables, release the PCIe slot's locking mechanism, and gently pull the card out of the slot.

- **Install New Components:** Install the new components, following the instructions provided with the hardware and the relevant chapters in this book. For example, to install a new CPU, you'll need to remove the CPU cooler, carefully lift the old CPU out of the socket, align and insert the new CPU, apply thermal paste, and reinstall the cooler.

- **Connect Cables:** Make sure all necessary power and data cables are connected to the new components. Double-check all connections to ensure they are secure.

- **Manage Cables:** Use zip ties or Velcro straps to tidy up any loose cables and maintain good airflow within the case.

- **Power On and Test:** Reconnect the power cable, turn on the power supply, and press the power button to start your PC. Verify that the new components are detected in the BIOS/UEFI and the operating system.

- **Install Drivers:** Install the latest drivers for your new components. You can usually download these from the manufacturers' websites.

- **Test for Stability:** Run stress tests and benchmarks, as described in Chapter 21, to ensure that your system is stable with the new hardware. Monitor temperatures and watch for any signs of instability or errors.

Upgrading Specific Components: Tips and Considerations

Let's delve into some specific considerations for upgrading common PC components:

1. Graphics Card (GPU)

- **Power Requirements:** Make sure your power supply has enough wattage and the necessary PCIe power connectors for your new graphics card.

- **Physical Size:** Check that your case has enough clearance to accommodate the length and thickness of the new card.

- **Driver Installation:** It's generally recommended to completely uninstall your old graphics drivers before installing the new ones. You can use a utility like Display Driver Uninstaller (DDU) to ensure a clean removal.

- **Monitor Compatibility:** If you're upgrading to a significantly more powerful GPU, make sure your monitor can take advantage of its capabilities. For example, if you're upgrading to a card capable of 4K gaming, you'll want a 4K monitor to see the full benefit.

2. Storage (SSD/HDD)

88. **Cloning vs. Clean Install:** If you're replacing your primary storage drive, you can either clone your existing installation to the new drive or perform a clean installation of the operating system. Cloning is faster and preserves your existing data and settings, but a clean install can sometimes offer better performance and stability.

89. **M.2 NVMe SSDs:** If you're upgrading to an NVMe SSD, make sure your motherboard has a compatible M.2 slot that supports the NVMe protocol. Some older motherboards may only support SATA-based M.2 drives.

90. **Data Migration:** If you're adding a new storage drive alongside your existing one, you'll need to decide how to allocate your data between the drives. You might want to move your operating system and frequently used applications to the faster drive for improved performance.

3. RAM

79. **Compatibility:** Ensure that the new RAM modules are compatible with your motherboard in terms of type (DDR4, DDR5), speed, and capacity. Consult your motherboard's QVL (Qualified Vendor List) for a list of tested and approved RAM modules.

80. **Mixing RAM:** While it's sometimes possible to mix RAM modules with different speeds and timings, it's generally not recommended. For optimal performance and stability, it's best to use identical modules, preferably from a matched kit.

81. **Dual/Quad Channel:** Make sure to install your RAM modules in the correct slots to take advantage of

dual-channel or quad-channel configurations for improved memory bandwidth.

4. CPU

59. **Socket Compatibility:** If you're upgrading your CPU, you'll need to make sure it's compatible with your motherboard's socket. In some cases, you may be able to upgrade to a newer CPU within the same socket generation. However, major upgrades often require a new motherboard.

60. **BIOS Update:** Before installing a new CPU, you may need to update your motherboard's BIOS to the latest version to ensure compatibility. Check your motherboard manufacturer's website for instructions on how to update the BIOS.

61. **Cooler Compatibility:** If you're upgrading to a significantly more powerful CPU, you may need to upgrade your CPU cooler as well. Make sure your cooler can handle the TDP (Thermal Design Power) of the new CPU.

5. Power Supply (PSU)

68. **Wattage:** If you're upgrading multiple components or adding a more power-hungry GPU or CPU, calculate your system's new power requirements and make sure your PSU has enough wattage to handle the load.

69. **Connectors:** Ensure that your PSU has the necessary connectors for all your components, including the appropriate number of PCIe power connectors for your graphics card.

70. **Efficiency:** Consider upgrading to a more efficient PSU (e.g., 80 Plus Gold or higher) to save on energy costs and reduce heat output.

Future-Proofing: Planning for Longevity

While it's impossible to predict the future of technology with certainty, there are some steps you can take to make your PC more "future-proof" and delay the need for upgrades:

44.   **Invest in a Good Motherboard:** The motherboard is the foundation of your system, and choosing a high-quality model with plenty of features and expansion options can provide more flexibility for future upgrades. Look for motherboards with multiple PCIe slots, M.2 slots, and support for the latest CPU and RAM technologies.

45.   **Consider Overclocking:** If you're comfortable with the risks and complexities, overclocking can help you extend the lifespan of your CPU and GPU by squeezing out extra performance.

46.   **Choose Components with Upgrade Paths:** When selecting components, consider their potential for future upgrades. For example, choosing a CPU socket that's likely to be supported for several generations can make it easier to upgrade your CPU without replacing your motherboard.

47.   **Don't Skimp on the Power Supply:** A high-quality, high-wattage power supply can provide a solid foundation for future upgrades, ensuring that you have enough power and the necessary connectors for new components.

48.   **Stay Informed:** Keep up with the latest technology trends and product releases. This will help you make informed decisions about when and how to upgrade your system.

Upgrading your PC can be a rewarding experience, allowing you to improve performance, add new features, and extend the lifespan of your system. By carefully planning your upgrades, researching compatibility, and following the proper installation procedures, you can ensure a smooth and successful upgrade process.

Remember to test your system thoroughly after each upgrade and monitor its performance over time.

With the knowledge and skills you've gained from this book, you're now well-equipped to build, maintain, and upgrade your own PC. As technology continues to evolve, you'll be able to adapt and enhance your system to meet your changing needs and enjoy the benefits of a custom-built machine that's tailored to your specific requirements.

CHAPTER TWENTY-FIVE: Maintaining Your PC: Cleaning and Optimization

You've built your PC, installed the operating system, drivers, and software, configured your BIOS/UEFI, and even explored the world of overclocking. Your system is running smoothly, and you're enjoying the performance and customization that comes with a self-built machine. But your journey doesn't end here. To keep your PC running at its best for years to come, you need to perform regular maintenance.

In this chapter, we'll cover the essentials of PC maintenance, focusing on two key aspects: cleaning and optimization. Cleaning involves physically removing dust and debris from your system's components and ensuring proper airflow. Optimization involves tweaking software settings, managing startup programs, and performing other tasks to keep your operating system and applications running smoothly. By following the guidelines in this chapter, you'll learn how to keep your PC in top shape, prevent potential issues, and maximize its lifespan.

The Importance of Cleaning: Dust, Heat, and Performance

Dust is the নীরব killer of PCs. Over time, dust can accumulate on your components, clogging fans, heatsinks, and other vital parts. This buildup can lead to several problems:

1. **Reduced Cooling Performance:** Dust acts as an insulator, trapping heat and preventing it from dissipating effectively. This can cause your components to run hotter, leading to thermal throttling, reduced performance, and potential instability.

2. **Increased Noise:** As dust accumulates on fans, they may need to spin faster to maintain the same level of airflow, resulting in increased noise.

3. **Component Damage:** In extreme cases, excessive dust buildup can cause short circuits or contribute to the premature failure of components.

4. **Aesthetics:** Let's face it, a dusty PC just doesn't look good. If you have a case with a window, you'll want to keep the interior clean and presentable.

Cleaning Tools: Assembling Your Kit

Before you start cleaning your PC, gather the following tools:

- **Compressed Air:** A can of compressed air is essential for blowing dust out of hard-to-reach areas, such as heatsink fins, fan blades, and tight corners.

- **Soft-Bristled Brush:** A small, soft-bristled brush, such as a paintbrush or a makeup brush, can be used to gently loosen stubborn dust.

- **Microfiber Cloth:** A lint-free microfiber cloth is useful for wiping down surfaces and removing dust from larger components.

- **Screwdriver:** You may need a screwdriver to remove panels or components for cleaning.

- **Isopropyl Alcohol (90% or higher):** This can be used to clean thermal paste off the CPU and cooler or to remove stubborn grime.

- **Cotton Swabs:** These are helpful for cleaning tight spaces or applying isopropyl alcohol.

- **Vacuum Cleaner (Optional):** A vacuum cleaner with a hose attachment can be used to remove large amounts of dust from the case, but be careful not to use it directly on components.

Cleaning Your PC: A Step-by-Step Guide

- **Power Down and Unplug:** Turn off your PC, switch off the power supply, and unplug the power cable from the wall outlet. Disconnect all peripherals as well.

- **Ground Yourself:** Wear an anti-static wrist strap or touch an unpainted metal part of the case to discharge any static electricity.

- **Open the Case:** Remove the side panel(s) of your case to access the interior. Depending on your case design, you may need to remove screws or release clips.

- **Remove Loose Dust:** Use a can of compressed air to blow out loose dust from the case. Start from the top and work your way down, paying particular attention to fans, heatsinks, and any areas where dust has accumulated. Hold the can upright and use short bursts of air.

- **Clean the Fans:** Use compressed air to blow dust off the fan blades. You can also use a soft-bristled brush or a cotton swab to gently clean each blade. If the fans are particularly dirty, you may need to remove them from the case for a more thorough cleaning.

- **Clean the Heatsinks:** Use compressed air to blow dust out of the heatsink fins. For stubborn dust, you can use a soft-bristled brush or a cotton swab dipped in isopropyl alcohol. Be careful not to bend the fins.

- **Clean the Graphics Card:** Pay special attention to the graphics card, as its fans and heatsink can accumulate a lot of dust. Use compressed air and a soft brush to clean the cooler shroud, fans, and any exposed heatsink fins.

- **Clean Other Components:** Use compressed air and a microfiber cloth to clean other components, such as the RAM modules, storage drives, and the motherboard. Be gentle and avoid using excessive force.

- **Clean the Case:** Use a vacuum cleaner with a hose attachment to remove dust from the bottom of the case and any filters. Wipe down the interior and exterior of the case with a microfiber cloth.

- **Reassemble and Reconnect:** Once everything is clean, reassemble your case, reconnect all peripherals, and plug the power cable back in.

Cleaning Frequency: How Often is Enough?

The frequency at which you need to clean your PC depends on several factors, including:

- **Environment:** If you live in a dusty area or have pets that shed a lot, you may need to clean your PC more frequently.

- **Case Design:** Some cases are better at filtering out dust than others. Cases with good dust filters may require less frequent cleaning.

- **Usage:** If you use your PC heavily or for demanding tasks like gaming or rendering, it may generate more heat and accumulate dust more quickly.

As a general rule, it's a good idea to clean your PC every 3-6 months. However, you should also keep an eye on your system's temperatures and listen for any unusual fan noise, as these can be signs that a cleaning is overdue.

Software Optimization: Keeping Your System Running Smoothly

In addition to physical cleaning, regular software maintenance is essential for keeping your PC running smoothly. Here are some key areas to focus on:

- **Operating System Updates:** Make sure your operating system is up to date with the latest patches and updates. These often include performance improvements, bug fixes, and security enhancements. In Windows, you can configure automatic updates through the Windows Update settings.

- **Driver Updates:** Keep your drivers up to date, especially for your graphics card, motherboard chipset, and network adapter. You can usually download the latest drivers from the component manufacturers' websites or use driver update utilities provided by the manufacturers.

- **Application Updates:** Regularly update your installed applications to the latest versions. This can improve performance, add new features, and address security vulnerabilities.

- **Startup Programs:** Over time, you may accumulate programs that automatically start when your PC boots up. Too many startup programs can slow down the boot process and consume system resources. In Windows, you can manage startup programs through the Task Manager (Ctrl+Shift+Esc) under the "Startup" tab. Disable any programs that you don't need to start automatically.

- **Disk Cleanup:** Windows includes a built-in Disk Cleanup utility that can help you free up space by removing temporary files, old system files, and other unnecessary data. To access it, search for "Disk Cleanup" in the Start menu.

- **Defragmentation (HDDs Only):** If you're using a traditional hard disk drive (HDD), you may need to periodically defragment it to optimize file layout and improve performance. SSDs do not require defragmentation. Windows includes a built-in defragmentation tool that can be accessed by searching for "Defragment and Optimize Drives" in the Start menu.

- **Malware Scans:** Regularly scan your system for malware using a reputable antivirus or anti-malware program.

Windows includes Windows Defender, which provides basic protection, but you may want to consider a more comprehensive third-party solution.

- **Uninstall Unused Programs:** Periodically review your installed programs and uninstall any that you no longer need. This can help to free up storage space and reduce clutter.

- **Registry Cleaning (Use with Caution):** The Windows Registry is a database that stores settings and configurations for your operating system and applications. Over time, it can become cluttered with obsolete or invalid entries. While some users advocate using registry cleaning utilities to optimize performance, these tools can sometimes cause more harm than good if not used carefully. If you do decide to use a registry cleaner, make sure to back up your registry first and only use reputable software.

- **System Monitoring:** Use system monitoring tools like Task Manager, Resource Monitor, or third-party utilities like HWMonitor to keep an eye on your system's performance, resource usage, and temperatures. This can help you identify potential issues and optimize your settings.

Creating a Maintenance Schedule: Staying Proactive

To ensure that you don't neglect your PC's maintenance, it's a good idea to create a schedule and set reminders for yourself. Here's a sample schedule you can adapt to your needs:

Monthly:

91. Check for and install operating system updates.

92. Check for and install driver updates, particularly for your graphics card.

93.   Run a quick malware scan.

94.   Review startup programs and disable any unnecessary ones.

95.   Use Disk Cleanup to remove temporary files.

Every 3-6 Months:

82.   Physically clean the inside of your PC, as described earlier.

83.   Check for and install application updates.

84.   Defragment HDDs (if applicable).

Annually:

62.   Perform a thorough review of installed programs and uninstall any you no longer need.

63.   Consider running a full system backup.

64.   Evaluate your hardware and consider potential upgrades.

Troubleshooting Performance Issues: Identifying and Solving Problems

Despite your best maintenance efforts, you may still encounter performance issues from time to time. Here's a systematic approach to troubleshooting:

71.   **Identify the Symptoms:** Pay close attention to the specific symptoms you're experiencing. Is the system slow overall? Are certain applications crashing or freezing? Do you see any error messages?

72.   **Check for Recent Changes:** Think about any recent changes you've made to your system, such as installing

new hardware, updating drivers, or installing new software. These changes could be the source of the problem.

73. **Monitor System Resources:** Use Task Manager or Resource Monitor to check your CPU usage, RAM usage, disk activity, and network activity. Look for any processes that are consuming an excessive amount of resources.

74. **Check Temperatures:** Use monitoring software to check your CPU, GPU, and other component temperatures. Overheating can cause performance issues and instability.

75. **Run Diagnostics:** Windows includes built-in diagnostic tools, such as the Memory Diagnostic Tool and the System File Checker, which can help identify and fix certain issues.

76. **Search Online:** If you encounter a specific error message or problem, search online for solutions. There's a good chance that someone else has experienced the same issue and found a fix.

77. **Consider System Restore:** If the problem started recently, you can try using System Restore to revert your system to an earlier state before the issue occurred.

78. **Seek Help:** If you're unable to resolve the issue yourself, don't be afraid to ask for help. Online forums, tech support communities, and the support websites of your hardware and software vendors can be valuable resources.

Conclusion

Maintaining your PC is an ongoing process that involves both physical cleaning and software optimization. By regularly removing dust, updating your software, and monitoring your system's performance, you can ensure that your PC runs smoothly, efficiently, and reliably for years to come. Remember that prevention is often better than cure. By taking a proactive approach to maintenance, you can avoid many common issues and enjoy a trouble-free computing experience.

As you continue to use and upgrade your PC, you'll undoubtedly learn more about its inner workings and develop your own personalized maintenance routines. Don't be afraid to experiment with different settings and tools to find what works best for your system and your usage patterns. And always remember that the PC building and maintenance community is a vast and supportive one. Whether you're a seasoned enthusiast or a first-time builder, there are countless resources and knowledgeable individuals ready to help you along the way.

With the knowledge and skills you've gained from this book, you're now well-equipped to build, maintain, and enjoy your own custom PC. Embrace the journey, keep learning, and never stop tinkering. The world of PC building is constantly evolving, and there's always something new to discover. Happy computing!